THE REPRODUCTIVE SYSTEM

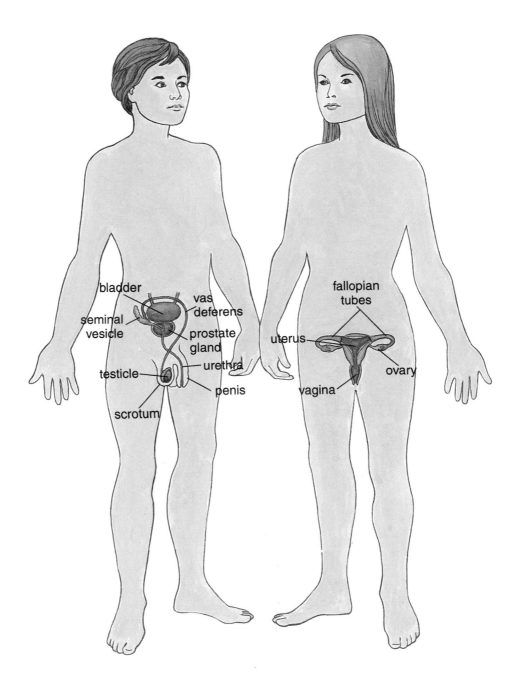

The Reproductive System

HUMAN BODY SYSTEMS

THE REPRODUCTIVE SYSTEM

Dr. Alvin, Virginia, and Robert Silverstein

TWENTY-FIRST CENTURY BOOKS
A Division of Henry Holt and Company
New York

Twenty-First Century Books
A Division of Henry Holt and Company, Inc.
115 West 18th Street
New York, NY 10011

Henry Holt ® and colophon are trademarks of
Henry Holt and Company, Inc.
Publishers since 1866

Published in Canada by Fitzhenry & Whiteside Ltd.
195 Allstate Parkway, Markham, Ontario L3R 4T8

Library of Congress Cataloging-in-Publication Data
Silverstein, Alvin.
Reproductive system / Alvin, Virginia, and Robert Silverstein.
p. cm. — (Human body systems)
Includes index.
1. Human reproduction—Juvenile literature. [1. Reproduction. 2. Sex instruction for children.] I.
Silverstein, Virginia B. II. Silverstein, Robert A. III. Title. IV. Series.
QP251.5.S55 1994

612.6—dc20   94-25912
                                                              CIP
                                                              AC

ISBN 0-8050-2838-2
First Edition 1994

Printed in Mexico
All first editions are printed on acid-free paper ∞.
10 9 8 7 6 5 4 3 2 1

Drawings by Lloyd Birmingham

Photo Credits

Cover: Howard Sochurek/The Stock Market
p. 9: David M. Phillips/Photo Researchers, Inc.; p. 10: Dr. Tony Brain/Science Photo Library/Photo Researchers, Inc.; p. 11(l): A.B. Dowsett/Science Photo Library/Photo Researchers, Inc.; p. 11(r): Jeff Lepore/Photo Researchers, Inc.; p. 13: Dr. Jeremy Burgess/Science Photo Library/Photo Researchers, Inc.; p. 15: E. R. Degginger/Photo Researchers, Inc.; p. 17(t): John Giannicchi/Science Source/Photo Researchers, Inc.; p. 17(b): Biophoto Associates/Photo Researchers, Inc.; p. 18: Craig J. Brown/Liaison International; p. 19: Ken M. Higheill/Photo Researchers, Inc.; p. 20: Ron Austing/Photo Researchers, Inc.; p. 23(t): The Royal Collection/Her Majesty Queen Elizabeth II; p. 23(b): ARCHIV/Photo Researchers, Inc.; p. 35: Prof. P. Motta/Dept. of Anatomy/University "La Sapieza", Rome/Science Photo Library/Photo Researchers, Inc.; p. 36: Professors P.M. Motta and J. Van Blerkom/Science Photo Library/Photo Researchers, Inc.; p. 41: CRNI/Science Photo Library/Photo Researchers, Inc.; pp. 45 and 52: Petit Format/Nestle/Science Source/Photo Researchers, Inc.; p. 49: James Stevenson/Science Photo Library/Photo Researchers, Inc.; p. 54: Blair Seitz/Photo Researchers, Inc.; p. 59: Blair Seitz/Photo Researchers, Inc.; p. 61: Richard Shock/Liaison International; p. 63(t): St. Bartholomew's Hospital/Science Photo Library/Photo Researchers, Inc.; p. 63(b): Gunther/Photo Researchers, Inc.; p. 68: Paul R. Kennedy/Gamma Liaison; p. 69(t): Jim Weiner/Photo Researchers, Inc.; p. 69(b): Jeff Isaac Greenberg/Photo Researchers, Inc.; p. 70: Richard Hutchings/Photo Researchers, Inc.; p. 71(l): Ursula Markus/Photo Researchers, Inc.; p. 71(r): Bill Truslow/Liaison International; p. 78: CNRI/Science Photo Library/Photo Researchers, Inc.; p. 80: NIBSC/Science Photo Library/Photo Researchers, Inc.; p. 81(l): Eamonn McNulty/Science Photo Library/Photo Researchers, Inc.; p. 81(r): Gamma Liaison; p. 82: SIU/Photo Researchers, Inc.; p. 86: R. Watts/Gamma Liaison; p. 88: Alexander Tsiaras/Science Source/Photo Researchers, Inc.

CONTENTS

SECTION 1

REPRODUCTION IN THE LIVING WORLD

A mosquito hovers over a puddle, laying tiny eggs that will soon hatch into wriggling larvae. An acorn buried and forgotten by a squirrel in the fall sprouts into a sturdy seedling the following spring, while the squirrel, snug in her nest in a hollow tree, is giving birth to a litter of tiny, hairless babies. Eels swim across the ocean to lay their eggs in the same rivers where they were born. And in homes and hospitals all over the world, each moment of every day, human mothers are giving birth to babies, too. Mosquito larvae, oak seedlings, squirrel pups, and all the other living creatures that are constantly appearing on the earth have a parent or parents. Many will themselves be parents someday. The ability to give birth to more of their own kind is called **reproduction**. It is found among all the living creatures of the earth and is one of the most important things that sets living creatures apart from nonliving matter.

All of the systems of the body work together to keep an organism alive and healthy—all except the reproductive system, that is. The reproductive system has nothing to do with keeping us alive; its function is to keep a species, or kind of living creature, alive. All living things eventually die. New creatures of the same kind must be born and grow up to take their place. Reproduction allows a new, younger living organism to be created out of part of older ones.

If any species of plant or animal suddenly became unable to reproduce, then all of that kind would disappear from the earth. For when all the creatures of that species grew old and died, there would be no new generation to take their place.

With the many different kinds of life in the world, it is surprising that there are only a few basic ways in which living things reproduce. The tiniest single-celled creatures, such as bacteria, merely split in two. The parent disappears and there are two offspring in its place. Other creatures, such as tiny yeast cells, reproduce by growing little buds that turn into small copies of themselves. In these forms of reproduction there is only one parent. They are examples of **asexual reproduction**.

But for nearly all of the larger animals and plants (and many of the smaller ones, as well), there must be two parents for reproduction to take place. These parents are of different sexes: one is a male and the other is a female. This type of reproduction is known as **sexual reproduction**. Insects, fish, birds, and all of the mammals (including humans) reproduce sexually.

In sexual reproduction, each parent forms a special kind of sex cell called a **gamete**. When the male gamete and the female gamete join, the life of a new creature begins. From that tiny single cell, a new organism begins to grow. When it is finished developing, the new creature may be an insect, a kitten, or a human baby, made up of trillions of cells.

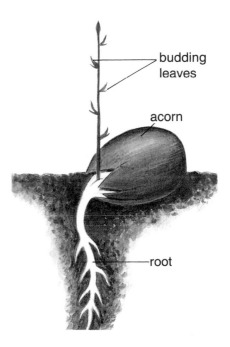

budding leaves

acorn

root

An acorn is produced when pollen from an oak tree male flower fertilizes a female flower. The acorn contains everything needed to sprout into a new oak tree.

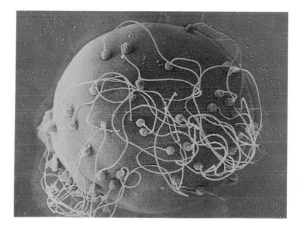

A human male gamete is called a sperm. Here, many sperm attempt to penetrate an ovum, which is a female gamete. Only one sperm will succeed in fertilizing the ovum.

REPRODUCTION WITHOUT SEX

Reproduction is an amazingly efficient way for living creatures to make sure that more of their kind will continue to exist. As long as there is enough food, warmth, moisture, and space, organisms like bacteria, for example, grow and reproduce. In about 20 minutes a single bacterium pinches in the middle, then splits into two bacteria. Each is a daughter bacterium and looks exactly like the other. Both of them look like their parent (which no longer exists), but they are only half the size.

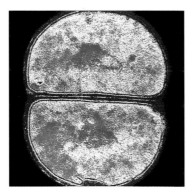

A bacterium dividing into two daughter cells

Now the two new bacteria feed and grow. Within 20 minutes or so, they, too, are ready to divide. Then there are four. After three hours there would be about 1,000 offspring. By seven hours there would be more than a million bacteria. In just one day, the mass of bacteria would weigh about 2,000 tons. Before the second day was over, the mass of bacteria would weigh more than the earth itself!

Of course, this could never happen, because the bacteria would run out of food and living space. But this example does show us that living things have enormous possibilities for making more of their own kind. (Even a pair of mice could have more than 100,000 descendants in about a year, if conditions were just right.)

Bacteria reproduce by a process called **binary fission**. A single cell splits to form two halves, which are usually identical. Most of the cells of our bodies also reproduce by dividing in half.

Some animals, such as tiny flatworms, break into several parts, and each part grows into a new adult. This is called fragmentation.

Another way that organisms can reproduce without sex is **budding**. A single-celled creature that reproduces by budding is the yeast. The yeast powder that you can use to bake bread is really made up of millions of tiny living yeast cells. When a yeast cell reaches a certain size, a little bud begins to grow on its edge. The little bud may break away from the parent and go off to lead a life of its own. It will live and grow and eventually produce its own buds. Or the little bud may stay attached to its parent and grow there until it is ready to have a bud of its own. In a while there may be a whole colony of yeast cells, growing together. Some sponges grow this way to form huge colonies.

Many plants can also make more of their kind without sex. Potatoes can reproduce somewhat like budding yeast cells. Tiny buds, called eyes, are formed on the tuber (the part we eat), which is actually a swollen stem. If you carefully cut out a small wedge of potato around an eye and plant it in soil, you can grow a whole new potato plant.

Strawberries send out long stems called runners, which grow along the ground, and every now and then send roots into the ground and form new strawberry plants. If the runner is cut or broken, the new plant can live on its own. One of the reasons why crabgrass is such a persistent weed is that it can send runners underground, which send up new shoots. So when the parent plant is torn out, the new shoots will give rise to even more weeds.

Some plants and animals reproduce by a method called **sporulation**. One-celled structures called spores are released and each one grows into a complete copy of the parent. Mushrooms reproduce by this method.

A yeast cell (left) reproduces by budding. A mushroom (right) releases spores, which will grow into exact copies of the parent plant.

SEXUAL REPRODUCTION IN THE PLANT WORLD

With asexual reproduction, new children are always exactly like their parents. In sexual reproduction male and female parents each give the offspring some of their traits, so that the new generation is a little different from the last. This variation helps a species to adapt to a changing world.

Creatures that reproduce sexually usually have special reproductive organs to produce the next generation. Flowers, for example, are often very beautiful, but they also have an important job to do—they are the plant's reproductive organs.

In some plants, such as willow trees, each individual plant is either male or female. A single willow tree could never make seeds that would grow into new willows; there must be two trees, one male and one female, for new willows to be born.

Some plants, such as corn, have two different kinds of flowers, male and female, both growing on the same plant. But most plants have what are called perfect flowers, each one containing both male and female organs. The male and female organs of the flower are usually in the middle of a sort of bowl, formed by the petals.

The male organs of the flower are called **stamens**. A stamen usually has two parts: a long thin stalk, or filament, and a rounded swelling on the top, called the anther. It is here that the dusty **pollen**, containing the male sex cells, called **sperm**, is produced.

The female organs of a flower are called **pistils**. A pistil is usually shaped like a vase, with a rounded **ovary** at the bottom, a thin neck, called the style, and a widened top, called the stigma.

The ova, or egg cells, of the plant grow inside the ovary. If these ova

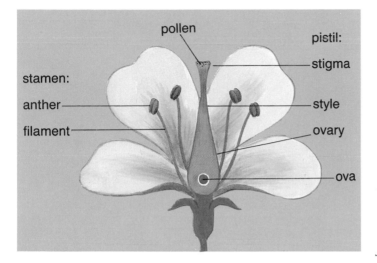

Most plants have flowers that contain both a male organ (stamen) and a female organ (pistil).

are ever going to develop into a new plant, they must be **fertilized**, or **pollinated**—sperm from pollen of the same species must join with them.

In plants with perfect flowers, pollen from the anthers may sprinkle down onto the stigma of the same flower. This is called self pollination. But plants that grow from seeds fertilized by pollen from the same flower, or even other flowers of the same plant, often are not as healthy and strong as when mating takes place between two different plants. This is true of animals, too, which is the reason why there are laws preventing brothers and sisters from marrying each other in human societies.

Many plants are pollinated by the wind. Breezes blow pollen off the anthers of a flower and across the fields or gardens until it comes to rest on the stigma of another flower. Animals, too, help to pollinate plants. When a bee lands on a flower to collect nectar and pollen, pollen grains are caught in the silky hairs of her body. When the bee visits other flowers, the pollen brushes

As a bee gathers pollen, she will deposit the pollen in a basket on her knee.

off and sticks to their stamens. A flower's colors, shape, and fragrance help to attract insects and animals.

Once the pollen has been deposited on the stigma, it must travel down to the ovary for fertilization to take place. The pollen grains begin to sprout like a seed. But instead of a root, a thin pollen tube grows down through the style. The male sex cells move down the pollen tube and divide to form sperm. When the tube grows into the ovary, the sperm fertilize the ova and a seed begins to develop.

A ripened seed contains a tiny embryo—a miniature plant with a root that will grow into the new plant's root system and a shoot that will form its stems and leaves. It also contains stored food on which the embryo will live until it is big enough to make its own food. Both the embryo and the stored food are wrapped in a seed coat, which will protect it from injury and keep it from drying out.

While the seed is ripening, the ovary develops into a fruit. The fruit may be soft and juicy, like a tomato or an orange. Or it may be dry and hard, such as nuts and the grains of cereal grasses. Sometimes a number of

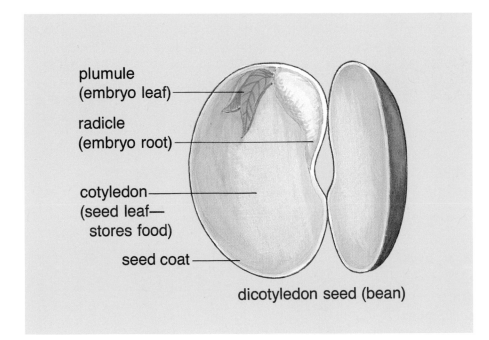

A ripened seed contains a tiny embryo.

ovaries from one or several flowers grow together to form fruits such as raspberries or pineapples.

The fruit contains nourishing food, but the seed embryo never uses this food at all. The fruit is formed to attract animals that will eat it and carry the seeds far from the mother plant. In that way the seeds are spread out so that the new plants will not crowd one another.

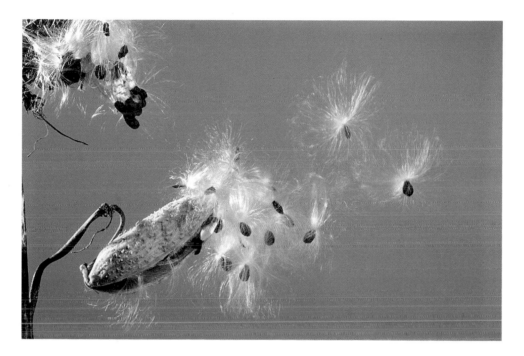

A milkweed pod explodes and sends its seeds to be carried on the wind.

Other fruits aren't good to eat but also help seeds to be scattered about. Cockleburs have spines and barbs that stick to an animal's fur or skin if the animal brushes against them. The maple seed has wings to help it fly through the air in the breezes, and the dainty parachute of the dandelion seed works in a similar way. Coconuts can float well and are carried along by rivers and oceans. Some fruits, like witch hazel pods, even explode, shooting their seeds out and away from the mother plant.

SEXUAL REPRODUCTION IN THE ANIMAL WORLD

Male and female animals of the same kind come together to reproduce, or mate. They are drawn together in many different ways. Pairs of lions, mice, and moths are brought together by special odors that the female gives off when she is ready to mate. Male birds sing a song to announce that they have a home ready for their mate-to-be. Male fireflies use their "living lanterns" to attract a mate as they fly overhead.

In animals, the male and female gametes are usually very different from each other. The female gamete is called an **egg**. It contains half of a complete set of plans to form the new organism. The egg also holds a supply of food, called **yolk**. Eggs come in all sizes, from a tiny speck too small to see without a microscope to a giant ostrich egg, 8 inches (20 centimeters) long. The egg is much larger than the male gamete, the sperm. The egg cannot move actively, but the sperm can. The sperm usually looks like a tiny tadpole, with a head and a long, lashing tail—all too small to be seen without a microscope. It swims along, wriggling and lashing its long, thin tail, as it travels to the egg. The sperm, too, contains half a complete set of plans for the new organism. When the egg and the sperm join together, the two halves of the plan combine to start the formation of a new creature. This developing unborn creature is called an **embryo**.

Some animals have just a few young at a time. Others have dozens, hundreds, or even thousands. Bears, horses, and humans usually have one or two babies. Mice and rats may have litters of a dozen or so. A fruit fly and a green turtle each may lay 200 eggs at a time. A pair of oysters send millions of eggs and sperm out into the water, where thousands of them join to form baby oysters.

In spite of their enormous differences in shape and size, the members of the animal kingdom are surprisingly similar in the structures that make

A micrograph of a human egg cell, which is really only about a tenth of a millimeter in diameter.

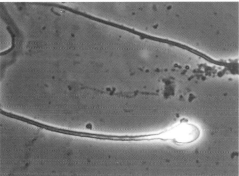

A human sperm is much smaller than an egg and has a long tail that propels it.

the gametes and the ways they come together. Sperm are produced inside the bodies of the males in structures called **testes**. Eggs, sometimes called ova, are formed in structures called ovaries in the body of the female.

Among many animals that live in the water, both the eggs and the sperm are sent out into the water in which the animals live. There they meet and join to begin a new life. Fish, frogs, oysters, and starfish reproduce this way. But this type of reproduction, called external fertilization because it happens outside the body, is rather chancy. The sperm and eggs are so tiny, and there is so much water, that many of them never find each other at all. Even after fertilization has taken place there are many enemies about that can eat up the embryos. So external fertilization is not a very effective system. If any of the young are to survive, enormous numbers of eggs and sperm must be produced.

Some of the fish, reptiles, birds, insects, and mammals have a more efficient way of getting their eggs and sperm together. Fertilization takes place inside the female's body. In this internal fertilization, the sperm swim through watery fluids in a channel inside the female's body to reach the eggs. Fewer eggs and sperm are needed to produce young.

Most reptiles and birds and many fish have internal fertilization, but their young do not develop inside the mother's body. Instead, they lay eggs in the water, on the ground, or in a nest that the parents may have built themselves. Heavy outer shells protect these eggs. Each one must contain enough food to feed the developing embryo until it hatches—once an egg is laid, there is no way to put in any additional supplies.

These turtle eggs were fertilized inside the female's body. They were laid in this nest on land, where they will hatch without any help from the parents.

In most mammals the fertilized egg develops inside the mother's body, and a special organ called a **placenta** provides nourishment for the growing embryo. The baby is born after it is fully formed. Marsupials, such as kangaroos and koalas, do not have a placenta, and their young are born before they are fully developed. The marsupial embryos finish maturing in a protective pouch on the mother's abdomen. They get their nourishment in the form of milk, secreted through the nipples inside the mother's pouch.

Marsupial young are born before they are fully developed and must finish growing inside their mother's pouch. The young opossums shown here are one week old. Each is about the size of a kidney bean.

Among the members of the animal kingdom, reproduction follows a general pattern: the more efficiently fertilization occurs and the better protection the developing young receive, the fewer eggs and young need to be produced. For example, a human female releases only a single egg each month, but a female frog releases millions of eggs each year. The young that are born through external fertilization receive little or no nourishment or protection from their parents. Animals that are produced through internal fertilization have fewer young, and the young that are born cannot survive on their own. They are dependent on their parents for food and protection from danger. As they grow, they learn how to take care of themselves.

UNUSUAL FORMS OF REPRODUCTION

A number of insects, such as aphids, honeybees, and wasps, can reproduce without mating. The mother lays eggs or bears living young, which develop in much the same way as the ones produced by normal sexual reproduction. But the mother does not mate, and her eggs are not fertilized. In some mysterious way, the eggs suddenly being to develop all by themselves and all the children are females. This odd form of reproduction is called **parthenogenesis**.

When a female wasp lays her eggs, she may or may not fertilize them with sperm she has stored in her abdomen. Fertilized eggs will become females. Unfertilized eggs will become males.

Most animals that reproduce by parthenogenesis can also reproduce sexually in the usual way, if conditions are right. Among the aphids, for example, during the spring and summer there are usually all females, which reproduce by parthenogenesis. But then as autumn approaches and the weather is getting colder, some males are born and mate with the females. The female aphids then lay special tough-walled winter eggs. These eggs can withstand the cold and snows of winter. They hatch in the spring into a new generation of females, who start the cycle over again.

Scientists have been able to produce a sort of parthenogenesis in the laboratory. By pricking unfertilized eggs of a frog with a needle or shocking them in some other way, they have made them begin to develop. Sometimes these unfertilized frog eggs develop all the way into full-grown frogs. Rabbits have also been raised in this way.

In humans, and in most of the other animals that we know well, there are two sexes—male and female—and the person or animal is either one or the other. But in some species, each animal is what is called a **hermaphrodite** and has sexual organs of both sexes. The term *hermaphrodite* comes from the names of the Greek god Hermes and the goddess Aphrodite. Snails are hermaphrodites, and so are many worms.

Some hermaphrodites reproduce by self-fertilization: two gametes produced by the same animal can fertilize each other. But most hermaphrodites must mate with another of their species. Earthworms, for example, have both testes and ovaries. When two earthworms mate, they line up with their heads in opposite directions and attach their bodies together in the middle, holding on tightly with tiny bristles and a slimy sort of glue. Each worm places sperm in a special sac inside the other worm's body. Then they part. The fertilized eggs develop into tiny earthworms. So, an earthworm can be both a mother and a father at the same time.

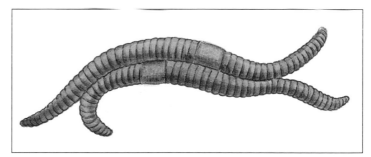

Earthworms mating

Some organisms actually change sexes. Male clam worms turn into females during the next season. The slipper limpet turns into a female if it meets a male slipper limpet or into a male limpet if its mate is female. Some tropical fish also change sex, depending on the conditions.

LEARNING ABOUT REPRODUCTION

The early humans had very little understanding of how children were conceived and born. Nor did they understand why children usually had some characteristics of their parents. It was believed that spiritual forces controlled the birth of a new life, and there were many superstitions to explain the process. The people who lived in northern Europe in ancient times believed that storks, which returned to their nests each year, brought the souls of unborn children to people's homes. A woman's monthly menstrual **periods** were widely regarded as a curse; in Biblical times, a menstruating woman was considered "unclean."

By about 2000 B.C., the ancient Egyptians had developed a simple pregnancy test that was 80 percent accurate! But Egyptian physicians believed that a woman's womb, or uterus, changed from one animal shape to another and could move around the body. Around 400 B.C., the Greek physician Hippocrates taught that both men and women produced semen, and after conception the woman's menstrual blood formed the child's flesh. A generation later, the Greek philosopher Aristotle said that male semen was guided by the spirit of the universe to produce a new life, which was merely nourished by the woman's menstrual blood.

In the second century A.D., the Greek physician Galen suggested that inside every woman there are tiny, fully formed embryos trapped in shells. Contact with a man causes the embryo to break out of the shell and start to grow. Another Greek physician who lived at that time, Soranus of Ephesus, was the world's first **gynecologist**, or doctor specializing in women's reproductive organs. He practiced in Rome, wrote a book on gynecology that was the standard reference on childbirth for the next 1,300 years or more.

In the late fifteenth century, Leonardo da Vinci based his drawings of human anatomy on careful observations and dissections. He was the first artist to show the correct position of the human fetus inside the uterus. In the sixteenth century several Italian physicians began to study and describe the parts of the female reproductive system. One of them was Gabriello Fallopio, who discovered the thin tubes that connect the ovaries to the uterus.

In 1677 the Dutch naturalist Antonie van Leeuwenhoek observed sperm cells under a microscope. Many of the scientists of his day believed that a tiny person was curled up inside each of the sperm cells.

In 1759 German anatomist Caspar Friedrich Wolff suggested that both parents were responsible for the development of a new baby. Scientists were able to observe the process of fertilization, the joining of a sperm with an egg cell, more than 100 years later.

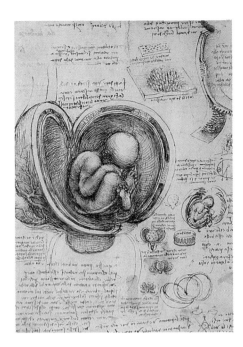

Leonardo da Vinci's drawing of a fetus in the uterus

Many advances were made during the last half of the nineteenth century. In 1856, an Austrian monk named Gregor Mendel began experiments with plants that showed that "factors" we now call **genes** are responsible for passing traits from one generation to the next. Mendel published his findings in 1866. In 1858 Charles Darwin proposed his controversial ideas about evolution. He believed that species or types of living creatures evolve, or change, to adapt to their surroundings because only the strongest survive to pass on their traits.

Since then science has made major leaps in understanding the reproductive system, as well as genes and heredity. This knowledge is helping to make childbirth and pregnancy safer, and is also helping those who are having difficulty conceiving children, or helping to prevent pregnancy for those who do not

Charles Darwin

wish to have children. By the 1970s, increased knowledge of genes blossomed into a new field of science called genetic engineering, in which scientists are able to manipulate the genetic blueprints that control living organisms. This has led to better ways of producing medications, as well as offering hope of curing many hereditary diseases.

THE MALE REPRODUCTIVE SYSTEM

The great advantage of internal fertilization is the direct transfer of sperm from the male to the female's body during mating; fewer eggs and sperm need to be produced because fewer of them are lost. In nearly all animals that reproduce through internal fertilization, the male has a special reproductive organ called the **penis**, which transfers sperm to the female. Penises are usually long and slim and fit neatly into a channel inside the female's body. The penis helps the sperm to find an egg by placing them deep inside, close to where the egg will be fertilized. Dogs, snakes, beetles, and even worms have penises. But a male bird has just an opening, which he presses over the female's reproductive, or **genital**, opening until they are stuck together by a sort of suction.

The long part of the penis is the shaft. The cap-shaped top of the penis is called the **glans**, which is Latin for "acorn." The sensitive glans is protected by a loose fold of skin called the **foreskin**. Many boys have the foreskin removed shortly after birth in a minor operation called a

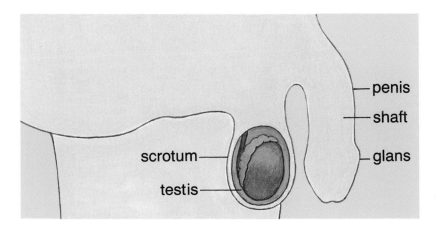

Sperm are produced in the testes, two small structures contained in the scrotum.

circumcision. Some doctors believe that circumcision helps to reduce infections in both men and their sex partners.

Sperm are not produced in the penis. They are formed in the testes, two small, egg-shaped structures that hang below the main part of the body, in a loose bag of skin called the scrotal sac, or **scrotum**. It might seem odd that these important reproductive organs are not protected inside the body, but there is an advantage to this arrangement. The normal body temperature is too hot to make sperm properly, but the temperature in the scrotal sac is about 3° to 5°F cooler than the rest of the body.

WHY IS IT COOLER IN THE SCROTAL SAC?

Heat a pot of water. When the water is warm, turn off the heat. Then take out a spoonful of the warm water. After a minute or two the water in the spoon is already cool, but the water in the pot hardly seems cooler at all. The pot, like the body, is very large and loses heat rather slowly. But the spoonful of water, like the scrotal sac, is much smaller and loses heat much more quickly. The scrotal sac does not cool all the way down to the temperature of the room because it is rather close to the warm body, and besides, its cells make some heat of their own.

Sperm are made in some 2,000 tiny coiled tubes called **seminifcrous tubules**, which are crowded inside the testes. If all these tubules were unraveled, they would stretch out for close to half a mile! An adult male produces more than 100 million sperm cells each day. They divide and divide again, gradually changing into mature sperm through a series of stages over a period of more than ten weeks. From the tiny tubes in the testes, the sperm travel into a larger collecting tube, called the **epididymis**, in which the sperm cells complete their maturing process. Mature sperm are the smallest cells in the human body—about 5,000 of them, laid out end to end, would measure only an inch (2.5 centimeters).

From the epididymis the sperm pass into the **vas deferens**, or sperm duct, in which they may be stored for several hours up to more than a

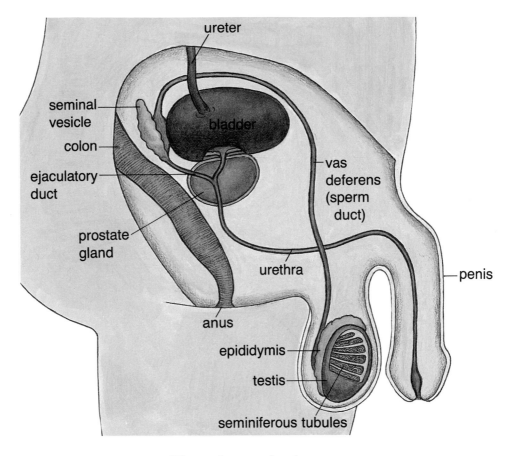

The male reproductive system

month. When a man is ready to place his sperm inside the body of a woman, the vas deferens leads the sperm upward to the penis. Then they pass into the **ejaculatory ducts**, tubes that lead through the **prostate gland**. On the way, the sperm are mixed with secretions from the prostate and several other glands, to form a milky white fluid called **semen**.

After leaving the prostate, the semen passes down the penis through a tube called the urethra. This tube also delivers urine from the bladder out through the penis. But urine and semen never pass out of the penis at the same time. Indeed, the sperm are very delicate and would be killed if urine touched them. Some of the chemicals contributed by the glands along the sperm ducts help to protect the sperm from any traces of urine that might remain in the urethra. Other substances in the semen provide nutrients for the sperm.

Normally, the penis is rather small and hangs down loosely. But it can swell up to a much larger size and become very firm and hard. It can do this because three cylinders of spongy tissue surround the urethra in the penis. When a man becomes sexually stimulated, the arteries to the penis enlarge. Blood rushes in, causing the cylinders to swell. This firming up of the penis, called an **erection**, helps in inserting it into the woman's reproductive tract.

THE FEMALE REPRODUCTIVE SYSTEM

A man's reproductive system is designed to produce male sex cells and deliver them to a female. But a woman's reproductive system is much more complicated. Not only must it produce female sex cells and receive the male sex cells, but it must also provide a place and nourishment for an embryo to grow, must allow the new baby to be born into the world, and must provide nourishment for the baby after it is born.

Both the penis and the scrotal sac of the man are outside the main part of the body. But the woman's genital organs are inside her body. Eggs are produced in two olive-shaped ovaries, which lie on each side of the pelvis. They are about the same size as the male testes. An egg is called an **ovum**, and it is smaller than a pinhead. It is the only human cell that can be seen without a microscope. A funnel-shaped structure with a fringe of fingerlike projections on the edge called fimbriae partly surrounds each ovary. This funnel is the entrance to one of the two **fallopian tubes**, or oviducts. Each tube is about 4 inches (10 centimeters) long.

When an egg is matured, it travels down one of the fallopian tubes to an upside down pear-shaped organ called the **uterus**, or womb. A fertilized egg develops into a baby inside the uterus, which contains the strongest muscle fibers in the body. This small organ, normally the size of a small pear, can stretch to many times its size to hold a baby 20 inches (51 centimeters) long.

The base of the uterus, the **cervix**, opens into a tube, about 3 to 6 inches (8 to 15 centimeters) long, called the **vagina**. The vagina has muscular walls lined with delicate mucous membrane, and it leads to an opening between the woman's legs. The man's penis is placed into the vagina during sexual intercourse, and the muscular walls can contract to grip the penis tightly. But during the birth of a child, the vagina acts as the birth canal, through which the baby passes out of its mother's body. Then the vaginal

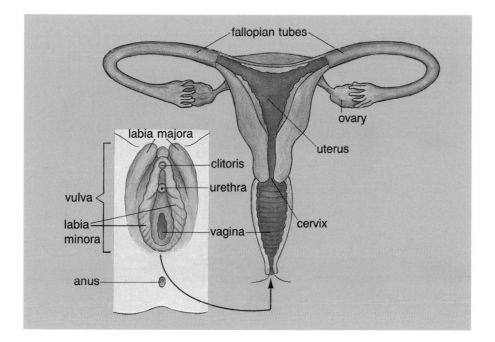

The female reproductive system

muscles relax, allowing the tube to widen to 4 inches (10 centimeters). The opening of the vagina is covered by the **hymen**, a thin sheet of tissue. The hymen may be broken the first time a woman has **sexual intercourse**, or during other activities such as horseback riding. In the male penis, the urethra is used to transport both sperm and urine. But in a female, the urethra is separate from the vagina. It ends in an opening in front of the vagina.

Two pairs of skin flaps called the **labia**, which means "lips," surround the vaginal opening. The outer pair have hair on the outside and oil and sweat glands inside. Another thinner set of flaps meet in front near the **clitoris**, a small pea-sized structure that looks like a miniature penis. The clitoris can expand in size during sexual excitement, like the penis, but it has no opening. The inner labia have many oil glands. A pair of glands found at the sides of the urethra and at the sides of the vagina secrete mucus for lubrication. The labia and the other external sex organs are called the **vulva**, which means "covering."

Breasts are also part of the reproductive system. After the baby is born, these organs secrete milk, a white fluid containing sugars, proteins, fats, and other nutrients to feed the growing child.

SEX HORMONES

Hormones are chemical messengers that control many activities in the body. Some help us to grow. Some help the cells of our bodies to burn food for energy. Still others, called **sex hormones**, help boys and girls to develop into men and women at a time in early adolescence called **puberty**. Hormones are made in special structures in the body called endocrine glands. These glands can be found clustered around blood vessels. Hormones slip through the vessel walls and into the bloodstream.

At puberty, the pituitary gland begins secreting hormones that cause the sex organs, the **gonads**, to begin secreting their own hormones. In a boy, male sex hormones, called **androgens**, are produced inside his testes. The most important of the androgens is **testosterone**. This male sex hormone is actually secreted even before a baby boy is born. It helps in the formation of his male sex organs. But then testosterone secretion stops, and it does not begin again until puberty.

At about twelve years old, an adolescent boy's testes begin to make testosterone, and many changes occur in his body. His voice deepens, and hair begins to grow on his chest, underarms, in his genital area (the area around his penis), and finally on his face. The testes begin to produce sperm, and his penis and scrotal sac begin to grow larger. In fact his whole body grows very rapidly at this time. Testosterone production continues through adulthood, which keeps the testes making more sperm.

The changes that gradually make a girl's body ready to bear children usually start when she is about eleven or twelve. Pituitary hormones stimulate the ovaries to produce female sex hormones, called **estrogens**. The shape of the girl's body changes as her breasts begin to grow larger and her hips become rounded. Patches of hair appear under her arms and in the genital area. The tiny oil glands in her skin may become too active at this time, producing worrisome pimples. But these will usually go away after the body settles down. The eggs in the ovaries begin to ripen, one by one each month.

Sex hormones continue to play an important role in a woman's life. Each month their production varies in a regular sequence, producing the **menstrual cycle**. Menstrual comes from the Latin word for "monthly." Hormones cause an egg to be released from one of the ovaries each month. Each month the hormones help to prepare the woman's body in case she becomes **pregnant**. If she does not, they start the cycle all over again.

When a woman does become pregnant, hormones play an important role in helping the unborn baby to grow, in childbirth, and in producing milk to feed a newborn baby.

Oddly enough, men's bodies produce some female sex hormones, and women's bodies produce some male sex hormones. But the hormones of the opposite sex are produced in much smaller amounts.

BE A CLEAN MACHINE . . .

Sweat and oil glands become more active during puberty. It is particularly important at this time to practice good hygiene to prevent pimples and body odor.

MENSTRUATION AND OVULATION

If you are a girl, you were born with as many as two million potential eggs in your ovaries. By the time you reach puberty, that number has decreased to only a quarter of a million or so. Each ovum must pass through certain changes before it is ready to join with a sperm to start a new life. Eggs begin maturing, one each month, after puberty. Only 400 to 500 of those eggs will ultimately mature, and very few will be fertilized.

A maturing egg cell grows and divides inside a tiny sac within one of the ovaries. This sac is called an **ovarian follicle**. It secretes the female sex hormone, estrogen.

When the ovum is mature, the follicle bursts open like a ripe seed pod, and the ovum pops out into the space inside the abdomen. This is called **ovulation**. Curving over each ovary is the open end of a fallopian tube. Tiny hairlike **cilia** within the tube wave back and forth, setting up a current in the fluids that fill the spaces around the ovary. The egg is drawn into the fallopian tube and travels through it toward the uterus. It is helped along by contractions of muscles in the walls of the tubes, much like the contractions that help move food along in the digestive tract.

Meanwhile, the ovarian follicle that burst changes into a small yellow structure called a **corpus luteum**, which means "yellow body." The corpus luteum begins to produce a new hormone, **progesterone**. This hormone does a number of things. It keeps a new follicle from forming, and it makes the lining of the uterus, called the **endometrium**, grow thicker.

The ripened ovum can only survive for a day or two. If the ovum has joined with a sperm by the time it reaches the uterus, it sticks to the inner wall, and there it develops into an embryo. But if the egg cell has not been fertilized, it breaks down. About ten days after ovulation, the corpus luteum stops making progesterone and shrivels up. Now that this special hormone is no longer being sent through the blood, the thick lining of the

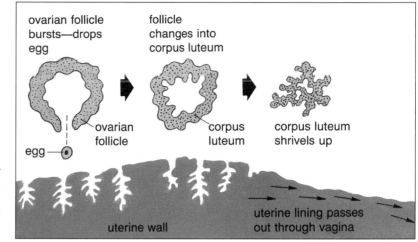

ovarian follicle
bursts—drops
egg

follicle
changes into
corpus luteum

egg ○

ovarian
follicle

corpus
luteum

corpus luteum
shrivels up

uterine wall

uterine lining passes
out through vagina

If an egg is not fertilized, the corpus luteum stops producing progesterone and the uterus sheds its lining.

uterus begins to break apart. After a while it passes out through the vagina in a flow of blood called the menstrual flow. This "monthly" cycle normally repeats about every 28 to 30 days, although its length can vary from 19 to 37 days. The blood flow, which is often called a period, usually lasts about four or five days.

Now a new follicle begins to develop in the other ovary, and the process beings again. About two weeks after the menstrual flow starts, a new egg pops out and begins its trip down a fallopian tube.

The cycle goes on, over and over again, except when a woman is pregnant—that is, carrying a child—and for up to six months after childbirth, if the mother breast-feeds her baby. Finally, when she is in her forties or fifties, her menstrual cycles will stop completely, and she will no longer be able to bear children.

Typically, menstrual cycles do not begin until an adolescent girl's body has laid down a large enough reserve of body fat (stored energy) to support a baby's growth. Losing a lot of weight, or engaging in regular strenuous exercise, may cause menstruation to stop temporarily.

Menstruation can be painful as the uterus contracts in spasms to remove menstrual fluid from the body. Some women suffer from irritability, depression, headaches, and bloating before or during their period. If the discomfort is severe, it is called **PMS** (premenstrual syndrome).

Monkeys and apes are the only animals that have menstrual cycles like human females. Many other mammals, including dogs, cats, and mice, have an **estrous cycle**. The female mates only at certain times of the year, when she is in heat.

INTERCOURSE AND FERTILIZATION

Perhaps someone has asked you if you would like to hear about "the birds and the bees," and then told you a bit about the facts of reproduction. Actually, the story of how birds and bees reproduce does not provide much useful information about human sex practices. A queen bee mates only once in her life (the poor drone that mates with her dies after his marriage flight), and birds do not even have penises!

In order for a sperm and egg to meet, two animals must have sexual intercourse. When animals have sexual intercourse we call it mating. But when humans have sexual intercourse we call it lovemaking. When humans have sex, usually there are feelings of love and intimacy between them.

During sexual intercourse, the man places his penis in the woman's vagina and moves rhythmically. Sensitive nerve cells in the skin of the penis transmit the sensations to the brain and spinal cord. A flow of hormones and nerve transmitters adds to the sexual excitement, until the sperm-carrying tubes in the man's testes and penis begin to contract, sending a little less than a teaspoonful (a few milliliters) of semen spurting out of the penis deep into the woman's vagina. This process is called **ejaculation**; the combination of the ejaculation and the intense feelings of pleasure and other emotions that go with it is referred to as an **orgasm**. The physical and emotional stimulation of intercourse can cause the woman to have an orgasm, too, with contractions of the vagina and intensely pleasurable feelings.

When the sperm enter the vagina, they swim upward in the watery fluids inside. Up they swim, through the cervix into the uterus and into the fallopian tubes. If an ovum is on its way from one of the ovaries, the egg and sperm will meet inside the fallopian tubes.

It is an exciting race. Hundreds of millions of sperm have entered the vagina. Many of them are gobbled up by large white blood cells in the walls of the vagina and uterus. About a million make it into the uterus, and just a few thousand get to the top of the uterus. But half of those that remain take the wrong turn and go up the wrong fallopian tube. Now the other half of the sperm are swimming toward the egg. A few hundred sperm will reach the egg, about an hour after intercourse.

The ovum is protected by a thick jellylike coating. A billion receptors—tiny docking points that fit the head of a sperm—are found on the egg's coat. When a sperm touches the egg, thousands of receptors hold it fast. A hundred or more sperm attach to the outer coat. The sperm are armed with a chemical that slowly eats away at the egg coat. Slowly the sperm burrow their way inside.

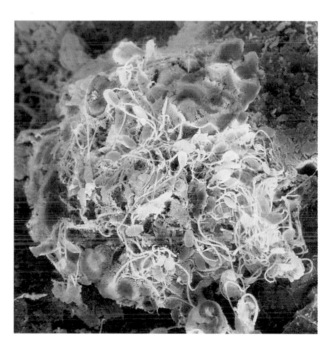

This egg is covered by numerous sperm. Only one sperm will succeed in penetrating the egg coat.

About six hours after they arrived at the egg, one of the sperm finally makes it through the egg coat. The cell membranes of the sperm and egg fuse, and the sperm leaves its own outer coat behind as it enters the egg. Immediately, the membrane covering the ovum thickens and forms a barrier around it. Tiny electrical changes in the egg's coat prevent any other sperm from getting inside. The nucleus of the sperm that made it, which carries half a set of plans for the new organism, joins with the nucleus of the egg, which also carries half a set of plans. Now all the information needed is there. The fertilized egg, or **zygote**, prepares to divide in two and start the process of development that will form a baby.

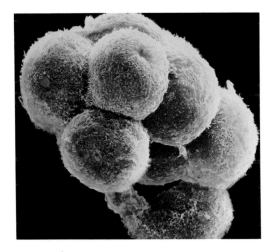

A micrograph of a zygote of 12 to 16 cells, taken about four days after fertilization

A woman does not become pregnant every time she has intercourse. In order for a zygote to be formed, a mature egg must be in the fallopian tube at the exact time when living sperm are there to meet it. But an egg is released from the ovaries only once a month. A day or so after it is released from the follicle, the egg dies and passes out of the body. If it meets a group of sperm in the uterus, this will be too late. The sperm, too, live only a day or two. So, unless a man and a woman have intercourse at just the right time of month, they will not be able to have a child. This fertile time usually occurs about two weeks after the start of the last menstrual period.

WHAT ARE THE CHANCES?

The chances were pretty slim that someone exactly like you would be born. The egg you came from was one of nearly a quarter million potential eggs. The sperm that fertilized that egg was one of several hundreds of millions.

THE MENSTRUAL CYCLE

Day 1 FSH (follicle-stimulating hormone) stimulates egg-bearing follicles to ripen. The cells in the follicle produce estrogen, which causes the lining of the uterus to grow thicker.

Day 10-12 There is a surge of estrogen, which tells the pituitary gland to release LH, luteinizing hormone.

Day 13 LH causes the follicle to rupture.

Day 14 Ovulation occurs—the egg is released and the follicle changes into the corpus luteum.

Day 15-25 The corpus luteum releases progesterone.

Day 26-28 If fertilization occurs, progesterone and estrogen prepare the uterus for pregnancy. If the egg is not fertilized, the corpus luteum breaks down and progesterone does not reach the uterus. The uterine lining begins to break down, causing menstrual flow.

Most women's cycles, however, are not perfectly regular, so it is possible for a woman to get pregnant at any time during her cycle. Women have gotten pregnant even during their periods!

There are other forms of intercourse that do not result in fertilization. **Homosexuality** involves sexual activity between members of the same sex. In this case, oral and anal intercourse are commonly practiced.

ABOUT THOSE BEES . . .

The females of some animal species have the unusual ability to store sperm in a special storage sac inside the abdomen. These sperm are let out as they are needed to fertilize eggs, sometimes as long as years after mating. The queen bee, for example, mates only once in her life—during her marriage flight. As she flies up from the hive, the male bees or drones fly after her. The strongest and fastest drone catches the queen and mates with her. Then the queen returns to the hive. She now has a lifetime supply of sperm stored away, and for as long as five years she will use them to fertilize her thousands of eggs.

SECTION 2

GENES AND HEREDITY

We inherit many of the characteristics that make us who we are. The color of our hair, skin, eyes, and how tall we can grow are hereditary traits that we inherit from our parents. Traits are passed on from one generation to the next in our genes. Half our genes came from our mother and half from our father.

Genes are complicated biochemicals that provide the pattern, or instructions, for building and operating a living organism. The different ways the chemical building blocks are arranged in genes determine the differences between species and between individuals of the same species. Bacteria have genes that we don't, and we have genes that bacteria don't, but all these genes are made from the same set of chemical building blocks, using the same kind of "spelling rules"—the genetic code is a universal language.

Genes are made up of a substance called DNA, or deoxyribonucleic acid. DNA is made up of even simpler chemicals that are strung together like a spiral ladder. The genes themselves are strung together into long, threadlike **chromosomes**. The chromosomes are found in the nucleus, which is the central control center, of body cells. Every cell in our bodies, except red blood cells, contains a nucleus, and so each cell has a complete copy of the chromosome instructions that make us who we are. Each cell, whether it is a nerve cell, muscle cell, or bone cell, contains the same DNA instructions. But in a nerve cell, for example, only the genes that concern the life and work of nerve cells are "turned on."

Humans have 46 chromosomes (23 pairs) inside each cell nucleus. However, sex cells—eggs and sperm—contain only 23 single chromosomes. When sperm and egg join together, the fertilized egg has the correct number of chromosomes for humans—46.

The study of heredity—the way genes work—is called **genetics**. You have 23 *pairs* of chromosomes, which means that you have two genes for

AMAZINGLY COMPACT INSTRUCTIONS

The DNA instructions in each nucleus are contained in a tiny dot too small to see. The coded instructions are about equal to the amount of information in a 300-page book. But these instructions about how to build and operate a human are so complicated that it would take nearly all of the books ever written to describe all that goes on within us.

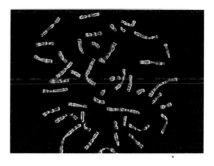

A set of human chromosomes

nearly every trait. Which one will determine what you look like? Some traits seem to be determined by just one gene of the pair, while the other seems to have disappeared. Genes like the brown-eye gene are said to be **dominant** over others. Their effects appear no matter what the other gene in the pair may be. That is why brown-eyed people sometimes have children with blue, green, gray, or hazel eyes. Although the parents' eyes were brown, they were also carrying a gene for another eye color. Such "hidden" genes are called **recessive**; their effects can be seen only if a person has inherited two of them, one from each parent.

Many hereditary diseases are caused by recessive genes. For example, one out of each 2,000 Caucasian babies will develop a hereditary disease called cystic fibrosis (CF). Yet in nearly all cases, both parents of each of these children seemed perfectly normal. Each parent was carrying a recessive CF gene, the effects of which were hidden by the dominant normal gene but appeared when the two recessive genes combined in their child.

For some traits, both genes have an effect. For example, people grow to be very tall, very short, and every height in between. The "tall" and "short" genes both contribute. (Actually, height, skin color, and a number of others traits are determined by not one but several different pairs of genes. At least eight pairs of genes determine skin color.)

Some of the traits that are passed on in our genes cannot be changed. But other traits depend on the environment as well as heredity. Your genes might provide you with a strong artistic ability, but if you are never given the opportunity to learn to draw or paint, your talent might never develop. The American-born children of Japanese immigrants are usually much taller than their parents. The richer diet they ate during their childhood allowed them to come closer to their inherited potential height.

DIVIDING CELLS

Most body cells divide by a process called **mitosis**. Hours before a cell divides, the chromosomes are copied. Each chromosome is a double-stranded thread. When they begin to divide, the two strands unravel. Each single strand is copied, using materials that are floating inside the cell. The cell ends up with 46 double-stranded chromosomes, each held together with its original other half at the center by what looks like a knot, the centromere.

The cell also makes many other changes in preparation for dividing. Two cylinder-shaped structures begin producing tiny fibers, which push the cylinders apart until they are at opposite sides of the cell. The nucleus comes apart, freeing the duplicated chromosomes. Next, fibers begin to form out of the knots that hold the chromosomes together, and they are pulled by the fibers from the cylinders in a tug-of-war. The knots come undone, and one chromosome from each pair travels to each side of the cell. Pieces of the nucleus form around each set of chromosomes at opposite ends of the cell until there are two nuclei in the cell.

Fibers form around the middle of the cell, pinching it in as if it were a bag with a drawstring, until it is pinched all the way to form two separate cells.

A few hours after fertilization, the zygote that developed into you divided for the first time. Since then, trillions upon trillions of cells have divided in you, and almost every time a perfect copy of the DNA instructions was made. When the pattern of genes is miscopied, or if the chromosome breaks and is patched up in a different way, the instructions for the organism are changed.

Our genes contain evidence that all life descended from the same ancestor. Many human genes are very similar to genes found in fish, rep-

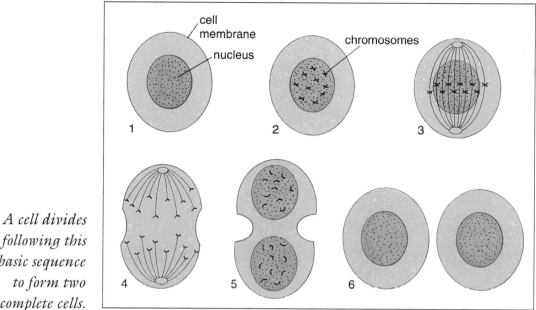

cell membrane
nucleus
chromosomes

1   2   3

4   5   6

A cell divides following this basic sequence to form two complete cells.

tiles, and other mammals, with just a few of the building blocks changed. We have some genes that are similar to those of insects and even bacteria. Tiny changes in the genes that are too small to produce a new species are responsible for the great variations among people. That is why no other person in the world is genetically exactly like you, unless you have an identical twin.

Sex cells do not divide by mitosis. If they did, each one would have the same number of chromosomes as its parent cells, and when they combined in fertilization their number would double. Imagine how many chromosomes people would have after a few generations of that! The male and female sex cells divide by a special process called **meiosis**. They divide twice, but the chromosomes are only duplicated once. That way a single spermatogonium (the first stage in sperm formation), for example, with 46 chromosomes, becomes four sperm cells, each with 23 chromosomes.

Sometimes chromosomes do not join up properly or are not copied correctly, resulting in a genetic disease. Down syndrome is an example of a birth defect caused by a mistake in the chromosomes, and cystic fibrosis is caused by changes in a specific gene, which scientists have recently identified.

HOW A BABY IS FORMED

For a time after fertilization, nothing much seems to happen. But then, suddenly, after about 30 hours, the single cell of the zygote splits in two. About 20 hours later, the 2 cells pinch in and split again, to form 4 cells. The splitting, or cleavage, occurs again, and 8 cells are formed, then 16, and 32, and 64. So far there has not been any growth—the many-celled embryo is no bigger than the original zygote.

As the cells divide, they stay clustered together like a berry. By the time the embryo has reached the uterus it has become a two-layered, fluid-filled hollow ball of cells and is called a **blastocyst**. About a week after fertilization occurred, the little embryo settles down in the lining of the uterus and buries itself in the rich, nourishing tissue. A net of fingerlike blood vessels fans out into the mother's tissues and soaks up nourishment for the growing embryo. This will develop into the placenta, which will bring the baby nutrition from its mother. The embryo is soon surrounded by the amnion, or **amniotic sac**, a sort of space capsule in which it will float in liq-

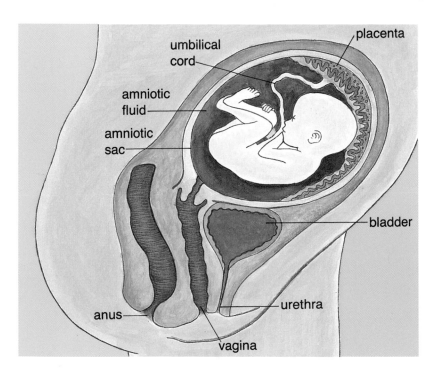

uid, protected from harm. It is suspended from the wall of the capsule by an **umbilical cord**.

At first the cells that were formed are all identical to each other. But then cells of different shapes, sizes, and functions are formed. Gradually the clump of cells begins to take shape. First it looks like a little rod. Then a bulge grows at one end and bends over. This will be the head. Another bulge appears below the head. This will be the heart, and it begins to beat at about four weeks.

It is hard to tell what the little creature will be like. It has a long tail and gill slits like a fish. It is only a quarter of an inch (0.6 centimeter) long, but it is 10,000 times heavier than it was when it was only one cell.

At about five weeks, little buds appear where the arms and legs will grow. The eyes are starting to develop, and the heart is beating stronger than ever inside the plump little belly. At this age there is very little difference between a human embryo and that of a donkey, rabbit, whale, bat, or lizard! But by the seventh week the embryo is starting to look human.

The embryo continues to grow. Fingers and toes are forming, and the body grows longer and covers the tail. About two months after the zygote was formed, the embryo is just about an inch (2.5 centimeters) long!

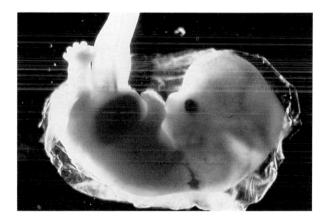

An embryo about seven weeks old
is beginning to develop toes.

IS IT A BOY OR A GIRL?

By nine weeks, the developing embryo is big enough to fit in a peanut shell. But nine weeks is an important turning point in the growing baby-to-be's life. Now you can tell what sex it will be.

A baby's sex is determined the moment an egg is fertilized. But for the first two months a growing embryo looks exactly the same whether it will be a boy or a girl.

A person's sex is determined by one of the pairs of chromosomes, called the **sex chromosomes**. A female has two X chromosomes. A male has an X and a Y. The pair of sex chromosomes divides when the sex cells are formed. The egg always carries an X chromosome, but a sperm can carry either an X or a Y chromosome. So if an X sperm fertilizes the egg it will be a female, and if a Y sperm fertilizes the egg it will be a male.

A very small part of the Y chromosome is responsible for making an embryo grow into a boy. Both sexes have the genes that provide patterns for making males and females. But a tiny part of a single gene in the Y chromosome acts as a switch to turn on the genes that will form a male.

The ovaries and the testes start out looking the same. But if the Y chromosome switches on certain genes, testes will develop. The testes start to produce male hormones, which cause the surrounding tissue to develop into male reproductive organs such as the penis, and prevent female reproductive organs such as the uterus and vagina from developing.

The part of the embryo that becomes the penis and scrotal sac in a male forms the clitoris and the vulva in a female.

Amazingly, by the sixth week, before the reproductive organs are finished developing into male or female organs, the cells that will eventually become eggs and sperm travel to where the ovaries or testes will form. They do not look like egg or sperm cells at all, but rather like jellylike amebas.

Some traits and diseases are sex-linked, which means they are associated with the sex chromosome. Pattern baldness and hemophilia, for example, are both associated with the X chromosome. However, they usually occur only in men.

THE ODDS OF HAVING A BOY OR A GIRL

You would think that the odds of a sperm carrying an X chromosome reaching an egg would be the same as for a sperm carrying a Y chromosome. But about 130 male embryos are formed for every 100 female embryos. Only 106 males are born for every 100 females, though. Scientists think that Y-carrying sperm may travel faster to the egg because the Y chromosome is lighter than the X chromosome.

In some rare cases a person's physical sex characteristics do not match his or her chromosome set, or a person may grow up feeling that he or she is trapped in a body of the "wrong sex." Such mixups are usually the result of hormonal influences before birth, which affect the development of the baby's body and brain. Hormones inside the mother's womb may also play a role in homosexuality, a preference for members of one's own sex as love and sex partners. But in recent years scientists have been finding evidence that genes help to determine a person's sexual orientation.

THE GROWING FETUS

By the ninth week the embryo is called a **fetus**. It has all the parts that are found in a human being, including genitals, fingerprints, and eyelids that close over its eyes. The proportion of body parts, however, is very different than it will be when the baby is born—the head of the fetus is about half the total length of the fetus! An adult's head is only about one-eighth the total length of the body.

From the beginning of the ninth week to the end of the twelfth week, the fetus nearly triples its size—to about 2.75 inches (7 centimeters) long. During the third month the trunk and limbs grow more quickly. Bone begins to form in the body. By the end of the third month, the fetus still weighs less than an ounce, but it can swallow, frown, and withdraw its leg if its foot is tickled.

A developing fetus's growth is often measured in **trimesters**—that is, the pregnancy is divided into three parts, of three months each. The second trimester begins in the fourth month. By then, the fetus looks much more human. Its eyes, ears, nose, and mouth are well-formed. Hair begins to grow on its head, and eyelashes and eyebrows appear. The heartbeat can be heard by a doctor with a stethoscope. By the end of the fourth month, the fetus is about 9 inches (22.5 centimeters) long, and the head is only a third of its total length. It can suck, drink, urinate, and defecate. The mother can often feel the baby moving between the sixteenth and eighteenth week, and during the fourth month the mother starts "showing" as her body bulges to make room for the growing fetus.

In the fifth month, the entire body of the fetus becomes covered with a coat of fine hair called lanugo. The skin is also coated with a waxy coating called vernix that keeps the skin from getting soggy. Its face is red and wrinkled, and its eyelids open and close. The fetus grows to about 12 inches (30 centimeters) long and weighs more than a pound (about half a kilogram).

By the end of the sixth month the fetus has completed the second trimester of its development. It is now about 14 inches (35 centimeters) long and weighs more than 2.2 pounds (1 kilogram). It may have a full head of hair, and the lanugo has largely disappeared. The fetus may frequently suck its thumb.

The final three months of pregnancy are a finishing off period. Fat deposits are laid out beneath the skin. The fetus sleeps and wakes up, kicks, startles, and sucks its thumb. It may turn many times before settling into a head-down position. At the end of the ninth month, about 266 days after conception, the average fetus weighs about 7 pounds (3.2 kilograms), measures 20 inches (51 centimeters) long, and is ready to be born. The baby has grown from a single cell to more than 6 trillion cells.

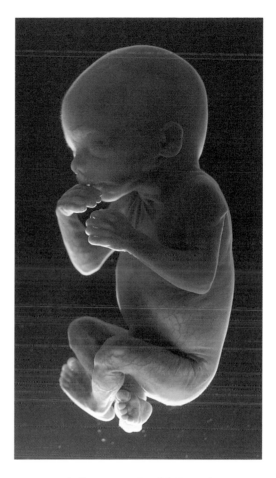

A five-month-old fetus is covered with fine hair.

THE WOMB WORLD

For months before it is born a fetus can hear sounds in the mother's body such as the heartbeat and intestinal rumblings, as well as the mother's voice, music, and other outside sounds. Two months before birth, the baby can also see inside the womb. Light filtered through the mother's tissues gives a reddish glow.

LIFE-SUPPORT SYSTEM

Before birth, every human being is a water animal. For nine months a human baby grows inside its mother, floating quietly in a liquid-filled chamber very much like a space capsule, which protects it from bumps and shocks.

The space capsule that protects the fetus is the amniotic sac. It is filled with amniotic fluid. The fetus swallows and breathes in the fluid, but it does not drown. It gets the oxygen it needs from its mother's body through the umbilical cord that attaches its abdomen to the placenta in the lining of its mother's uterus. The place where the umbilical cord attaches to the abdomen will become the belly button, or navel, after the baby is born.

The spongy placenta is formed from tissues from the fetus, but becomes closely linked with the mother's tissues as it grows into the lining of the uterus. The placenta makes chemicals that help the mother's body

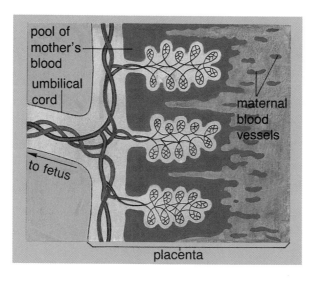

The mother's blood vessels in the placenta are completely separate from the blood vessels of the fetus.

make the changes necessary to accommodate the new life growing within her. The placenta grows along with the growing baby. When the baby is ready to be born, the placenta has grown to about 1 inch (2.5 centimeters) thick and 8 inches (20 centimeters) long.

The fetus does not need to eat, for sugars and other food chemicals flow in from its mother's body through the blood vessels coming from the placenta. Its body wastes flow out again through other blood vessels in the umbilical cord, and its mother's bloodstream carries them off. But its blood does not mix with its mother's at all. There are two sets of blood vessels in the placenta, the mother's and the fetus's. Although gases and other chemicals pass easily back and forth between them, the two blood-streams are completely separate.

Antibodies and other protective chemicals pass from the mother's blood to the fetus through the placenta. During the first few months after birth, these antibodies will protect the newborn from diseases such as smallpox, measles, polio, and other viruses against which the mother has built up immunity.

But harmful materials can pass to the fetus, too. The virus that causes German measles (rubella), for example, can harm an unborn baby. The **AIDS** virus, HIV, may pass through the placenta to infect the fetus. But many babies born to mothers with AIDS do not become infected. They test HIV positive at first, because they have received antibodies from their mothers, but eventually they lose these antibodies and give a negative HIV test. Drugs taken by the mother, such as alcohol and nicotine, can also pass to the fetus. When a pregnant woman smokes, for example, her fetus's heartbeat speeds up under the influence of nicotine.

PREGNANCY

A woman usually first suspects she is pregnant when she does not get her period on time. By then the fertilized egg has already developed into an embryo, and some of its organs are just starting to appear.

A pregnancy test will confirm whether or not a woman is pregnant. Home tests can be used to check the urine for a hormone that is produced only when a woman is pregnant.

As the embryo grows in the mother's uterus, the mother's body undergoes many changes to accommodate the new baby. Her body begins to look different, and it also has to work harder—to provide food and oxygen for the growing embryo in addition to supplying the mother's own needs.

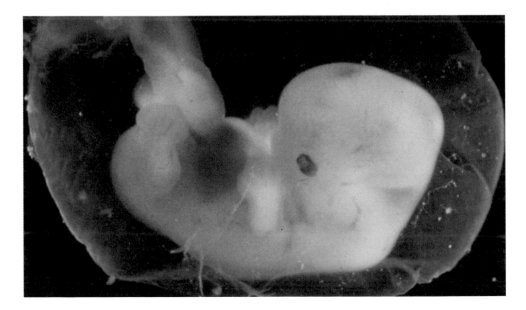

This five-week-old fetus has buds that will eventually become its arms and legs. The amniotic sac surrounds it.

During the early months of pregnancy, there may be little or no weight gain, but a pregnant woman will ultimately gain about 20 to 30 pounds (9 to 14 kilograms). The uterus will expand more than 20 times its normal size. The size of the breasts may double. Her blood supply increases by almost one-third, and the heart has to pump harder. Her respiration rate increases to provide more oxygen. The kidneys have to filter an increased amount of urine.

By the fourth month, the uterus can no longer fit into the pelvic cavity between a woman's hips. It expands upward into the abdomen. The abdominal wall stretches and sticks out more and more as the baby grows.

The growing womb presses on the mother's internal organs, making her feel uncomfortable. For example, because the womb presses on the bladder, a pregnant woman may have to urinate more often than usual. Her stomach can hold less food because it is squeezed by the womb, and constipation may occur because of pressure on the large intestines. It may be harder to breathe because the woman's organs are squeezed up into the chest cavity. Pregnant women often feel tired from the extra weight and strain.

Sometimes a pregnant woman may feel nausea, especially in the morning. This is called **morning sickness**, and it may be due to the increased secretion of hormones. Recent studies suggest that an increased sensitivity to foods that could be harmful to the fetus may be the cause of nausea and vomiting during pregnancy. Morning sickness usually goes away by the third month.

In order to be born, a baby must pass through a ring formed by the pelvic bones. These bones are normally held tightly together by strong ropelike ligaments. But shortly before birth, hormones make the ligaments stretch more than normal so that the baby will be able to pass through more easily. However, other ligaments also loosen, including those that support the spine. Combined with the extra strain due to the woman's increased weight, these changes may cause back problems late in the pregnancy.

During the pregnancy a woman usually visits an **obstetrician**, a doctor who specializes in delivering babies and caring for pregnant women, for regular **prenatal** checkups. These visits are important to make sure the pregnancy is going well, and that mother and unborn baby are healthy.

In the case of high risk babies, **amniocentesis** may be performed.

*Regular prenatal
checkups are important
to maintain good health
for both the mother and
her unborn baby.*

Amniotic fluid is removed from the amniotic sac using a hollow needle, and it is then tested for various genetic diseases and other possible problems.

Many women will have **ultrasound sonography**. High-frequency sound signals are bounced off the fetus to form a picture of the baby on a television screen or printout. The doctor can check the growing fetus and the uterus to make sure everything looks normal.

Pregnant mothers need to take care of themselves and eat well, because they have to provide nutrients for the growing baby in addition to themselves. There are many things that women must avoid during pregnancy to reduce the chances that problems will develop.

Women who smoke are more likely to have premature babies or babies who have a lower-than-normal birth rate. The babies' growth and intelligence may be stunted. In addition, miscarriages (losing the fetus before it is developed enough to be born), and complications during pregnancy and birth are more common.

Women who drink alcohol during pregnancy are at risk of having a baby with **fetal alcohol syndrome**, in which severe physical and mental defects may occur. Women addicted to drugs such as amphetamines, barbiturates, cocaine, and heroin run similar risks, but in addition, the babies may be addicted, too, and go through painful withdrawal during their first few days after birth. "Crack babies"—babies born to mothers who are addicted to the smoked form of cocaine—are typically very irritable and may suffer from long-lasting developmental problems.

Even prescription drugs like antibiotics used to treat bacterial infections can cause problems for the developing fetus. Years ago doctors prescribed a drug called thalidomide to prevent morning sickness. But some babies were born with flipperlike limbs that were not formed properly. Doctors learned that women should avoid most drugs during pregnancy, especially during the early months.

Viruses can also cause problems. If a woman gets German measles early in her pregnancy, the unborn baby's sight and hearing can be affected. Pregnant mothers must also avoid X rays.

A BABY IS BORN

The quiet life of the fetus changes very suddenly when the walls of its little world begin to shake and contract. The contractions grow stronger and more violent. They are slowly pushing it downward, head-first. The birth process is called **labor**. This name is fitting because labor is a lot of work for the mother. A woman usually goes through between 8 and 24 hours of labor for the first pregnancy and less for subsequent pregnancies. Labor pains, which occur when the strong-muscled walls of the uterus tighten or contract, often begin rather far apart and last less than 30 seconds. But gradually they come closer together and last much longer.

The mother's hip bones are moving apart, and the cervix opening is slowly widening, or **dilating**. The membrane sac in which the baby floats bursts open, and the fluid rushes out. The baby is pushed out into the world. The head usually emerges first and then the body follows. Finally the baby is born.

In a very short time the baby's body must make many important changes. For nine months it has been an underwater animal, constantly wet and warm, and it has received food and oxygen through an umbilical cord. As soon as the baby is born, the doctor quickly cleans fluid out of the nose and mouth. The cold air causes the baby to breathe, and its lungs begin to work for the first time. A valve in its heart closes, and the blood vessels that delivered blood in and out through the umbilical cord close, too. The heart now pumps blood to the lungs instead. Meanwhile, the umbilical cord is clamped and tied. Now the baby is not getting any more nourishment from the placenta. It will have to eat and get rid of waste products on its own. The air is colder than the fluid inside its mother's womb, and the baby's body must learn to keep its temperature steady. The baby cries for a moment and then looks around at the new world it has just entered.

Doctors believe that hormones play an important role in starting the birth process. **Oxytocin** is produced by the fetus and by the mother's pituitary gland. Labor probably starts when a certain level of this hormone causes the uterus to begin contracting. As the baby starts to descend into the pelvis its head presses against the cervix. This sends messages to the brain to release oxytocin. Hormonelike prostaglandins produced inside the uterus also help to stimulate contractions.

Usually women are given a pain reliever during childbirth because the pain during contractions may become unbearable. In the past, most women were often given a general anesthetic. They would wake up and find they had delivered a baby. Today, local anesthetics or sedatives are given to reduce the pain while still allowing the woman to take an active part in the delivery.

Many women prepare for childbirth by taking natural childbirth classes. Using techniques such as the Lamaze method can help to reduce the pain of childbirth. Special breathing and relaxation techniques help her to focus her attention away from the pain. A woman may choose someone close to her—husband, mother, friend—as her Lamaze coach.

In the United States, most women have their baby delivered at a hospital by an obstetrician. High-tech monitors often keep a careful watch on the fetus's heartbeat and respiration, while also recording the length and intensity of contractions during the delivery. Often women are connected to an IV tube that delivers liquid and nutrients directly into their blood stream so that they do not become dehydrated.

Today, parents may prefer more natural surroundings for the birth of their child. Some hospitals are making delivery rooms look more like a bedroom than an operating room. Many people are choosing to have their baby delivered by a specially trained nurse called a nurse-midwife at a special birthing center. Actually, around the world, more than three-quarters of the babies born each year are delivered by midwives. Some people are even choosing to have their babies delivered at home. Since most midwives are not doctors, the mother must be rushed to a hospital if complications develop.

BIRTH COMPLICATIONS AND PREMATURE BABIES

Pregnancy and childbirth are natural processes that a woman could do herself, if she had to. The doctor is really only there in case there are complications.

During the pregnancy a woman receives regular checkups to make sure everything is going well. Sometimes problems develop. Some women develop toxemia, a serious condition in which the mother's blood pressure rises to dangerous levels. Bed rest and a restricted diet may be enough to control toxemia. A woman may go into premature labor—the birthing process starts, but the baby is not developed enough to survive on its own if it is born. Sometimes drug therapy and bed rest can help keep the baby from being born until it is developed enough to survive.

Problems can develop during childbirth, too. Sometimes the delivery may not be going as quickly as it should be, and the baby or mother starts to have difficulty. The doctor may have to help the baby come out faster. Some doctors use forceps, which can help pull the baby forward. A vacuum extractor serves the same purpose and is used more frequently today. A suction cup is attached to the baby's head, and the baby is "vacuumed" out of the birth canal.

At some point during labor, the doctor or midwife may decide that the baby may not be able to pass safely through the birth canal. The baby may be too big, or the placenta may be blocking the baby's path, for example. Sometimes the baby may be in distress. It may not be getting enough oxygen. This could occur if the umbilical cord is pinched during the birth process. If these emergencies arise, the baby may have to be delivered by a **cesarean section**, or C-section. This is a major surgical operation in which a cut is made in the mother's abdominal wall and uterus, and the baby is removed.

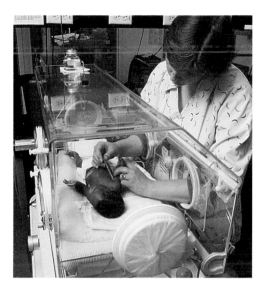

A premature baby usually finishes its development in an incubator, which provides a safe environment.

Babies usually come out headfirst. In a **breech birth** the feet or buttocks are the first to enter the birth canal. This makes delivery much more difficult and dangerous—the baby can suffocate before the head finally comes out. Sometimes a doctor can gently turn the baby around before labor begins. In the United States many breech babies are delivered by a cesarean section.

Babies that are born between 37 weeks and 42 weeks of **gestation** (prenatal development) are considered "term" babies—they have gone through the full time of pregnancy. Those born earlier are preterm or premature babies, and those born after their due date are postterm. Babies that weigh less than 5.5 pounds (2.5 kilograms) at birth are called low-birth-weight babies.

A premature baby looks thin because the fat layer that is laid down under the skin in the last two months has not formed yet. Its lungs may not be developed enough for it to breathe on its own and its body may not be able to keep warm. A premature baby is often placed in an incubator that keeps its body at the right temperature, supplies extra oxygen, and keeps the baby safe from germs. The incubator monitors the heart rate and breathing rate so that doctors and nurses can be alerted if problems arise. The incubator protects the baby just as if the baby were finishing its development in the mother.

A NEWBORN BABY

A newborn baby often looks funny. It is covered with a white greasy substance called **vernix caseosa**. It may have very little hair and may be wrinkled and puffy-eyed. Sometimes a newborn looks like it has a "banana head." A baby's skull can be bent out of shape during the delivery. But this is perfectly normal. There are gaps between the bones of a newborn's skull so that the head can be compressed somewhat and squeeze through the birth canal more easily. In a few days the head will be a normal shape.

In proportion to the rest of the body, a newborn baby's genitals are larger than they will be at any other time during childhood, until puberty. During the early months of life, the rest of the body will grow more rapidly, so that the genital organs will no longer seem oversized. In addition, the scrotum and vulva may be red and inflamed at birth, because the mother's hormones have crossed the placenta, causing temporary swelling.

As soon as a baby is born, it is given an Apgar score. This is an evaluation of its health based on heart rate, how well it is breathing, muscle tone, reflexes, and color. The baby is then cleaned off, drops are placed in its eyes to prevent infection, and it is wrapped to keep it warm. The baby needs extra wrappings to keep it warm until it is able to regulate its body temperature automatically. Often a baby will be placed at its mother's breast shortly after birth. Then the baby is bathed, weighed, and measured while the mother recuperates for a short while.

Newborn fish swim as soon as they are born. A newborn colt will be able to stand up just moments after birth. But human babies are pretty helpless. Babies sleep much more than adults. For the first day or two after birth, the baby is usually rather quiet and sleepy. It is still not quite used to the world. Rocking (like the swaying motions it experienced in the womb) and recordings of a human heartbeat will have a soothing effect. A newborn baby doesn't know how to control the muscles that move its hands or legs. It will take time to learn how to make its body do what the baby wants it to.

However, a newborn infant is able to do many things automatically without having to learn them. These reflexes are instincts that we are born with to help us survive. They are programmed into our genes and passed from one generation to the next. If you lay a finger in a newborn's hand, it will grasp the finger tightly. When the baby hears a loud noise, it may startle, throwing its arms out wide. It will blink if you touch its nose. A newborn can make walking movements when it is held in the air. A baby can't talk, but it can cry when it is hungry, cold, uncomfortable, or tired. If you touch a newborn's cheek, it will turn its head toward you and begin rooting—trying to find a nipple to suck. And, most important, the baby is born with a sucking reflex. Remember, it was already able to suck while it was still inside the uterus. It will suck on anything placed in its mouth—a finger or a nipple from a breast or bottle. Many of these reflex actions disappear within a few months. By then the baby has learned better how to use its muscles and can make voluntary movements.

An infant is born with a grasping reflex and will hold tightly to a finger placed in its hand.

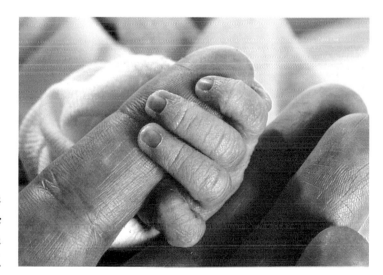

MULTIPLE BIRTHS

The birth of more than one baby at once is called **polyembryony**. The armadillo, for example, usually has four identical babies. Cats may have a half-dozen kittens at a time, which may not look at all alike. Rats and mice may have a litter of a dozen offspring. But among humans, polyembryony is rare.

Twins are born about once in every 88 births. Triplets are born only about once in every 8,000 births. Quadruplets (four babies born at once) occur once in each 650,000 births. And quintuplets (five babies) and sextuplets (six babies) are so rare that their births make the headlines. However, multiple births are more common in women who take special fertility drugs to help them become pregnant more easily.

The odds of having twins vary in different parts of the world. Twins are most common among those of African descent and least common in Eskimos.

When large numbers of babies are born at once, they are usually very small at birth because there is not enough room in the uterus. They also may not get enough nourishment because the mother's heart might not be strong enough to pump enough blood through many placentas.

Not all human twins, triplets, and other multiple births are identical. In fact, only about one set of twins in each three sets is a pair of **identical twins**. The others are nonidentical, or **fraternal twins**. All twins that are not of the same sex are fraternal twins. They develop from two different ova, which accidentally happened to be released from the ovaries at about the same time and were fertilized by two different sperm. The ability to have twins is thought to be inherited—some women may have a tendency to release two eggs at once.

Identical twins occur when the egg divides for the first time and the two daughter cells detach. If, when each of these daughter cells divides, the

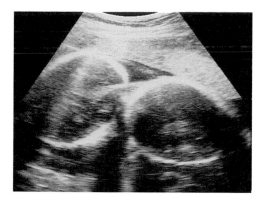

An ultrasound picture of the heads of twins in the uterus

new daughters do not remain attached, triplets or quadruplets may develop. If the split isn't complete, **Siamese twins** develop. These twins often share limbs and organs, so it may be hard to surgically separate them.

Fraternal twins have separate placentas, amniotic sacs, and umbilical cords. Identical twins share a single placenta, although they each have their own amniotic sac and umbilical cord.

When quadruplets are born, several different things could have happened. Four eggs may have been fertilized. Two eggs could have been fertilized and then split. Three eggs could have been fertilized and one split.

Identical twins (or higher multiples) share the same heredity. But remember that for many traits genes determine only the potential. So, identical twins, brought up in different surroundings, might grow up to be quite different. Studies of twins separated at birth and reared apart, however, have often shown surprising similarities not only in appearance but also in personality and behavior. In fact, twin studies are an important tool for scientists who are trying to determine how much our heredity contributes to our personality, susceptibility to diseases, and various other traits.

Identical twins have the same genetic makeup.

FOOD FOR BABY

A newborn baby cannot eat the foods that children or adults eat. The milk that is made in its mother's breast is all that it will need to grow for several months.

Males and females both have breasts or **mammary glands**, but hormones cause women's breasts to be different. At puberty, hormones from the ovaries cause fat tissue to accumulate around the breasts, and an extensive duct system begins to develop. During pregnancy, hormones cause the breasts to enlarge, and the duct system branches even more in preparation for delivering milk to the nipples when it is needed.

Estrogen and progesterone produced by the placenta prevent milk from being produced during pregnancy. But when the placenta is delivered from the body, these hormones no longer stop milk production. After childbirth, hormones control the production of milk. When the baby sucks on its mother's nipple, her brain causes prolactin to be secreted; this hormone stimulates milk production. Oxytocin is also secreted, causing milk to be released into the ducts leading to the nipples. The more the baby drinks, the more milk is produced.

Breasts are not involved in the actual reproduction process, but because of their important role in nurturing a new baby, and because milk production is controlled by hormones of the reproductive system, they are considered accessory organs of the reproductive system.

Within each breast there are 15 to 20 lobes that contain clusters of milk-producing glands. Tubes, or ducts, carry milk to the nipple. There are 15 to 20 tiny openings in the nipple for the milk to come out of. A circle of darker skin called the areola surrounds the nipple. Fat glands in the skin lubricate the areola to prevent chapping when the baby sucks. In addition to the milk-secreting glands, breasts are made up of fat and fibrous tissue to provide support, as well as a rich supply of blood vessels and nerves.

Breast milk is usually best for babies. It is at just the right temperature, it is sterile, and it carries antibodies that help babies fight colds and other illnesses. In addition, breast-feeding stimulates the secretion of oxytocin, which causes the mother's uterus to contract, helping it to return to a normal size faster.

Many women choose not to breast-feed their babies. Some women find it difficult to breast-feed. Others must use bottles because they have to go back to work. When babies are bottle fed, unless the mother uses a breast pump to produce supplies of breast milk, a special formula must be used. For young babies, cow's milk is not a good substitute for human milk, because it is very different. Human milk has more sugar and more fat than cow's milk. Human milk has less protein, but the proteins are different, and cow's milk does not have enough of some of the vitamins and minerals that human milk provides.

Modern formulas provide the same nutrition as breast milk, although they do not provide antibody protection. Bottle feeding has an advantage in that it also allows a father to become involved in the feeding, which may help strengthen the bond for the father and give the mother a chance to rest. Babies usually start to be weaned by six months, when they may begin to eat other foods.

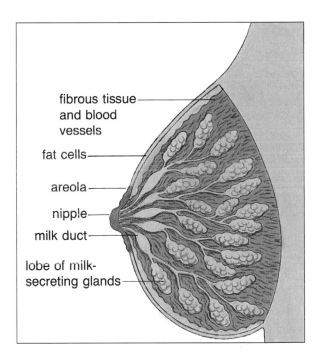

The structure of a female breast

SECTION 3

GROWING TO MATURITY

A fruit fly is fully mature in only a few days and lives only a month. A mouse becomes an adult in a few weeks and is old at a year and a half. Human babies take much longer to become adults, but we also live much longer.

It takes about 20 years for a human to become fully mature. Until that time he or she continues to grow both physically and intellectually. After adulthood physical growth stops, but learning continues.

Life after birth is often divided into five stages, although there is quite a bit of variation as to when these stages occur:

1. *The newborn or neonatal period* lasts from birth through the first few weeks of life. During this period the body has to adapt to a completely new environment.

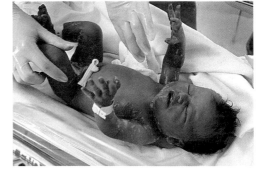

A newborn must get used to the sensations of a new environment.

2. *Infancy* begins at the end of the newborn period and continues through the end of the first year, when the infant usually can stand

alone and walk. A baby's first year is filled with major events. Gradually it begins to respond to the world around it—first to its mother's touch and voice, then shortly thereafter, to its father and to other humans and objects. A newborn has very little coordination. Steadily the infant gains control over its body, learning to focus its eyes, to reach and grasp with its hands, to turn over, sit, crawl,

A baby usually learns to sit up around six months of age.

stand, and finally to walk. The baby learns to communicate, first merely by crying, but then shaping experimental babblings into recognizable words. At the same time there is a steady physical growth, too. By the end of the first year a baby will triple its birth weight.

3. *Childhood* lasts from the end of infancy to puberty (the time of sexual maturation), which begins at about ten years of age in girls and about twelve in boys. Children grow steadily during this period at a rate of about seven pounds (three kilograms) a year. Baby teeth start to come in at about six months of age, and the first permanent teeth come in when the child is six or seven years old. Children usually become thinner and stronger as they grow taller. During childhood children depend on their parents to provide necessities, but slowly they learn the skills that will be needed to make it on their own when they have matured. By two years old, a

Childhood is a time when skills in many areas are developed.

child is very active and copies many things his or her parents do. Two-year-olds learn by trial and error and imitation; they can't think things out for themselves yet. At three the child is also curious, constantly asking questions. Four-year-olds can do numerous things for themselves—they can eat and dress themselves, for example. They know how they are expected to behave, and how to respond to situations. During the school years we learn more about our world. We continue to learn for the rest of our lives, but children learn more quickly and easily.

4. *Adolescence* begins with sexual maturation and extends through the teen years as intellectual and emotional maturity is gradually acquired. This period is considered to end at about nineteen in girls and twenty-one in boys. Puberty occurs at the beginning of adolescence. At this stage **secondary sexual characteristics** such as pubic hair and breasts grow, and the sexual organs become functional. Before puberty males and females look alike except for the genitals. But hormones cause other structural differences, which are secondary sex characteristics. Males' voices become deeper and their shoulders become broader; they have more body hair than females at this age, are taller, and their muscles become bigger and stronger. In females, the pelvis becomes wider and the layer of fat under the skin becomes thicker during adolescence, making females look softer.

Adolescence begins with puberty and is the first step toward adulthood.

5. *Adulthood or maturity* extends from the completion of adolescence until old age. The body is fully mature by early adulthood, but the aging process causes changes in the body to continue throughout adulthood.

Adulthood can extend from age twenty or so (left) well into old age (right).

CHANGING ON SCHEDULE

There is a great deal of natural variation in when puberty occurs—not only individual variations but also general patterns among different peoples and under different conditions.

Among American girls, breast buds first appear at an average age of about eleven years, usually followed by the growth of pubic hair. The first period occurs at about eleven to thirteen years. In boys the testes become larger and pubic hair begins growing at about age twelve on the average. The penis grows larger and underarm hair grows. Changes occur in a boy's voice during early puberty. Semen can be ejaculated by about thirteen and a half, but mature sperm are not usually produced until fourteen to sixteen years of age.

MENOPAUSE

From adolescence on, a man's body continues to produce sperm for the rest of his life, although the number of sperm produced does decrease with age. But a woman's reproductive system stops functioning when she is in her forties or fifties. This change is called **menopause**, and it may occur all of a sudden or gradually over time.

Just as hormones are involved in beginning the menstrual cycle of an adolescent girl, and continue to control her period throughout adulthood, hormones are also involved in the ending of the menstrual cycle. During menopause the ovaries stop producing progesterone and produce only tiny amounts of estrogen. This slows down the release of eggs from the ovaries, making a woman's period occur irregularly at first. Eventually the menstrual cycle stops altogether, so that a woman no longer has a period. When this happens she cannot become pregnant anymore.

Gradually the ovaries, uterus, and uterine tubes become smaller, and the ovarian follicles are replaced by fibrous tissue. The vagina shortens, narrows, and loses some of its ability to stretch.

Some women experience unpleasant symptoms during menopause. They may have "hot flashes"—hot tingling sensations over the whole body. They may experience headaches, dizziness, sweating, weakness, itching, nervousness, and an increase in blood pressure. Emotional depression may also occur. These symptoms can last for months or even years. Some women may need to be given hormone treatments. These treatments do not keep the reproductive system functioning, but they help to reduce the symptoms.

Treating women in menopause with estrogen hormones has caused a lot of controversy. Some doctors feel it increases the risks of breast and uterine cancer, but others insist that the treatment is perfectly safe, particularly when progesterone is also given. Estrogen replacement therapy after menopause helps to prevent **osteoporosis**, a thinning and weakening of the bones. Recent evidence suggests it may provide some protection against heart disease and also against Alzheimer's disease and other forms of mental deterioration that may occur during aging.

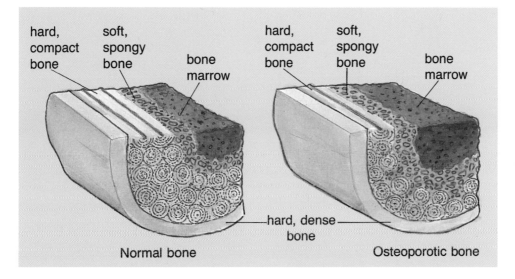

When osteoporosis occurs, normal hard bone becomes thin and weak as it is replaced by soft, spongy bone.

REPRODUCTIVE PROBLEMS

Some reproductive problems are caused by mistakes when sex cells form. A girl might be missing one X chromosome, for example, creating a 45-chromosome set with XO instead of the normal female XX. This female would have poorly formed genitals and at puberty would not mature. A male can be born with an extra sex chromosome, giving him an XXY. He has male genitals and male characteristics, but his reproductive system does not work properly and he is likely to be mentally handicapped. A controversy arose when it was pointed out that some criminals who had committed violent crimes were XYY males. Scientists suggested that the extra Y chromosome caused an increase in testosterone production, causing these men to be more aggressive. But some men with an extra Y chromosome are not violent.

Hormonal problems while a baby is developing inside the mother can cause odd reproductive problems. If the fetus's testes do not produce male hormones at the right time, female sex organs will form. The child looks like a female, but is really a male. If the mother has a tumor that secretes male hormones, a female fetus might develop male genitals. In both of these rare cases the person will not be able to have children. Even rarer are hermaphrodites, people with both male and female sex organs.

Male Reproductive Problems. A boy may be born with **hypospadias**, in which the underside of the penis did not close completely. Or he may have one or two undescended testicles. The testes are formed in the abdomen and normally drop into the scrotum before a baby is born. When the testes do not come down by themselves, they are brought down surgically after birth.

Men should periodically check their testes for bumps or other abnormalities. Cancer of the testicles is the most common cancer of men in their twenties and thirties. Two out of three men over seventy suffer from prostate problems. The prostate gland may be a site of cancer or bacterial infections. More often, it simply becomes enlarged. Since the prostate surrounds the urethra, enlargement can cause difficult and painful urination. Epididymitis is an inflammation of the epididymis, caused by a bacterial infection that travels from the urinary tract to the sperm duct.

A man may be **sterile**, that is, his body does not produce sperm, or he may have reduced fertility if not enough or abnormal sperm are produced. This may occur when the seminiferous tubules are damaged due to an

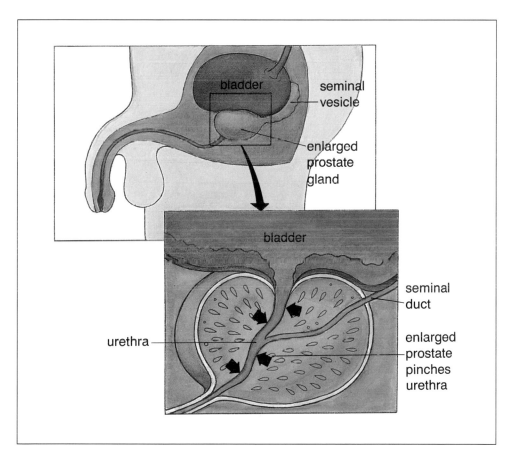

Older men often have prostate gland problems. An enlarged prostate gland can pinch the urethra and make urination difficult.

infectious disease (such as the mumps contracted during adolescence or as an adult), injury, dietary problems, alcoholism, or exposure to X rays. Sterility is different from **impotence**, in which a man is unable to maintain an erection due to physical or psychological problems and therefore is not able to have sex.

Female reproductive problems. The organs of the female reproductive system—ovaries, uterus, and breasts—are frequent sites for tumors and other growths. Many are harmless, but cancerous tumors are also common, particularly in women over forty. Breast cancer and cervical cancer are the two most common cancers among women of all ages. If lumps in the breasts or unusual bleeding or discharge from the vagina are detected early, the hopes for survival may be good. If not detected in time, the cancer can spread to other organs in the body. Regular self-examinations of the breasts, **mammograms** (X rays of the breasts), and regular **Pap smears** (a painless procedure in which tissue samples from the vagina and cervix are obtained during regular gynecological exams and examined under a microscope) have helped to lower the cancer death rates among women.

A woman with breast cancer may have a **mastectomy**, a surgical operation in which the breast and other tissue may be removed. Doctors are still debating whether the whole breast should be removed, or just the tissue containing the tumor, which is removed in a procedure called a lumpectomy. If cancer of the uterus is detected, a woman may have a **hysterectomy**, in which the uterus is removed. The ovaries and fallopian tubes may also be removed at the same time.

One of the strangest reproductive disorders is called **endometriosis**. A piece of endometrial tissue detaches from the lining of the uterus and grows somewhere else inside the body—around the rectum or appendix, for example. This piece of endometrium goes through the same monthly changes as the uterus does each month: it gets thicker, and then sloughs off and bleeds. Surgery may be necessary to correct this often painful disorder.

A woman may suffer from vaginitis—periodic yeast infections or bacterial infections in her vagina, which produce itching and large amounts of discharge. It is treated with creams, gels, or suppositories.

Toxic shock syndrome is a rare illness that occurs in some women who use tampons to absorb their menstrual blood flow. Caused by a bacterial infection that develops if the tampon is left in too long or is too absorbent, it produces high fever, vomiting, and sometimes severe shock.

Because of the complicated interaction of hormones and several different organs in the female sexual cycle, many things can go wrong causing **infertility**—the inability to conceive. One of the most frequent causes of infertility in women is a failure to release eggs each month. Infertility can also be caused by blockage of the fallopian tubes.

SEXUALLY TRANSMITTED DISEASES

Sexually transmitted diseases are a big problem all around the world. In the United States more than one million teenagers are infected each year—a quarter of all the new cases. Altogether, as many as fifty million Americans are affected. There are more than 25 sexually transmitted diseases (also called **STDs**, or venereal diseases), which are caused by many different organisms. The only similarity is that they are passed through various forms of sexual contact.

The most common STD in the United States is **chlamydia**, which is caused by a bacterium. The route of transmission is vaginal intercourse. In men and women a common symptom is frequent and painful urination. When a pregnant woman has chlamydia, her baby is at risk of developing an eye infection or pneumonia as it passes through the birth canal during delivery. Chlamydia can be successfully treated with antibiotics.

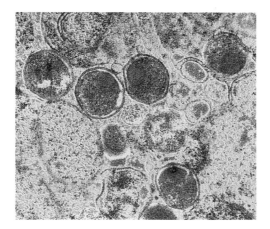

The pink spheres are chlamydia bacteria inside a human cell.

Gonorrhea is another common venereal disease caused by a bacterium. It is spread through vaginal and anal intercourse. This infection can spread through the reproductive tract, causing sterility as well as damaging other parts of the body such as the heart and kidneys. The bacteria cannot cross over the placenta to infect a fetus, but infection can occur during the birth process when the newborn passes through the birth canal. This is why antibiotic drops are placed into the eyes of every newborn after birth. Gonorrhea usually responds to a variety of antibiotics.

About one million women in the United States are treated each year for **pelvic inflammatory disease (PID)**. This STD is caused by several bacteria, particularly those that cause chlamydia and gonorrhea. The bacteria are transmitted during vaginal intercourse. Symptoms of acute PID include pain in the lower abdomen, vaginal discharge, fever, and nausea. A woman should not ignore early signs of the disease. If left untreated, PID can lead to infertility, primarily because it causes blockage of the fallopian tubes. It also puts an infected woman at risk for an ectopic, or tubal, pregnancy—a hazardous condition in which a fertilized egg starts to develop in a fallopian tube instead of in the uterus. PID is treated with antibiotics.

Another venereal disease that is causing growing concern is **genital herpes**, caused by herpes simplex virus type 2. Over 25 million people in the United States are infected with the virus. It can be transmitted by oral and vaginal intercourse. Similar to the herpes simplex virus type 1 responsible for cold sores, genital herpes produces painful blisters on the reproductive organs. This virus, which stays in the body for life, has been found to cause serious birth defects in children born to infected mothers and has also been linked with cervical cancer. Acyclovir is the drug used most often to reduce outbreaks of the disease. A new, promising therapeutic vaccine has been developed that also reduces the frequency of genital herpes outbreaks, but there is no cure for the disease.

Syphilis is caused by a corkscrew-shaped bacterium. It is spread by vaginal and anal intercourse. The earliest symptom is a chancre sore in the mouth or on the genitals. The fluid in the sore is very infectious. If antibiotic treatment is not given, years later serious damage may occur in the heart and blood vessels, lungs, and central nervous system. A pregnant woman with syphilis can pass the disease to her unborn child. Penicillin is given to treat the disease.

The newest, but most frightening STD of all is AIDS. This disease was first discovered in 1981, and by the end of 1993 more than 360,000 Americans had been infected. AIDS (*a*cquired *i*mmune *d*eficiency *sy*ndrome) is caused by the human immunodeficiency virus, HIV. In the United States, the virus is spread primarily by anal intercourse and by blood-to-blood contact, such as the sharing of infected IV needles, a common practice among IV drug abusers. It may also be transmitted through vaginal intercourse (the main transmission route in some parts of the world) or from an infected pregnant woman to her unborn baby. This virus attacks the white blood cells of the immune system, leaving a person unable to fight off other infections, which eventually causes death. There is no cure for AIDS, but researchers are working on a number of approaches. The FDA has approved use of four drugs to slow HIV reproduction.

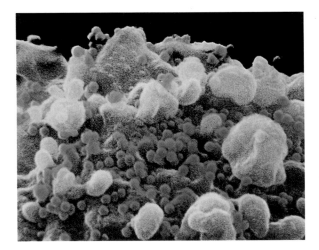

HIV, the virus that causes AIDS, has infected this white blood cell in the immune system.

Viral **hepatitis**, particularly the form caused by the hepatitis B virus, is spread in much the same ways as AIDS but is far more contagious. About half a million Americans are infected with hepatitis B or C, and many become carriers, able to transmit the virus to others even after they have recovered. The hepatitis viruses cause liver damage, and they can kill; worldwide, hepatitis B is the eighth leading killer, causing 1.2 million deaths each year. Hepatitis is treated with antiviral drugs. Some people are responding well to treatment with alpha interferon.

It is important to know about venereal diseases, but understanding their symptoms and treatments is not enough to prevent infection. The only sure way to prevent sexual diseases is to abstain from sex and intravenous drug use. The risks can be reduced by practicing safer sex—choosing a partner carefully, forming monogamous relationships (having only one sexual partner), getting tested for HIV and hepatitis if one has had previous partners, and using a latex condom every time while having sex.

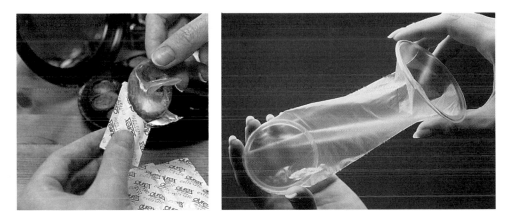

Using a condom every time during sexual intercourse will help prevent STDs. A latex condom for the male is shown at left. A condom for the female (right) is also now available.

TEEN PREGNANCY

Our society has many conflicting values concerning sex. Religions and traditional values teach us that sexual activity is something that should only be shared by a married couple. And yet peer pressure and the media—television, movies, books, music—give people the idea that sex can be okay outside of marriage.

Because of AIDS, a growing number of young people are thinking twice about having sex, or are at least taking precautions to prevent diseases and unwanted pregnancies. But the fact is many teens are still sexually active without taking precautions, and an alarming number become pregnant. Recent studies have shown that nearly half of teenage girls between fifteen and nineteen are sexually active, and there are about one million teenage pregnancies in the United States each year!

Often, a pregnant teen is not ready for motherhood. A doctor is one person who can help the teen through this difficult period.

There are many reasons why teenage parents and their babies may face special difficulties. Teenagers are usually not ready financially or emotionally to take on the responsibility of raising a child. But in addition, there are many medical reasons why teen pregnancies may be difficult. Babies that are born to teenage mothers are more likely to be premature or of low birth weight. In fact, babies born to teens have twice the chance of dying during infancy than a baby born to a mother in her twenties. Teenagers also have more complications during pregnancy.

Among animals, the only purpose of sexual intercourse is for reproduction. Much of the time, among humans, sex is regarded mainly as a way of sharing an intimate experience between two people who care greatly for each other. Pregnancy is often thought of as a risk that goes along with sex. Many teens do not know much about reproduction. With a better understanding of this important body system, teens would be able to make a more educated choice about their sexual activity and would have more control over when they become pregnant.

BIRTH CONTROL

In some religions, birth control is not allowed. But scientists say that the world is becoming too crowded with people. If the world population continues to increase at the present rate, in about 600 years there will be one person for every square foot of land area on the earth!

Devices or methods that allow people to have sex while reducing the chance of pregnancy are called **contraceptives**. One way to keep a baby from getting started is to keep the sperm from reaching an egg. This can be done by covering up the penis with a latex sheath called a **condom**. Another way to prevent conception is to cover the opening to the uterus with cup-shaped devices such as **diaphragms** and **cervical caps**, or to block the passage with a **vaginal sponge**. Creams, foams, or jellies containing chemicals that kill sperm are often used in combination with these devices.

One of the most popular methods of birth control is "the pill." Actually, there are several different kinds of **birth control pills**. They all contain hormones that send signals to the body's monitoring centers indicating that the woman is pregnant. That stops the secretion of the hormones that trigger the release of an egg from the ovaries. Pills may be a combination of estrogen and progesterone (or synthetic variations), or may contain only progesteronelike hormones. Some contraceptive pills are taken every day, and some for only part of the month. Hormones can also be implanted under the skin of the arm, enclosed in tiny tubes from which they slowly leak out into the tissues. Scientists are trying to develop a birth control pill for males.

Another birth control method is an intrauterine device, or **IUD**. A doctor can place a small plastic device inside the uterus of a woman who does not wish to have children. The IUD prevents an embryo from developing in the wall of the uterus. Some IUDs release tiny amounts of hormones or copper compounds, which also have a contraceptive effect. IUDs are used much less often than in the past because of several possible problems, including infections causing sterility, or pregnancies developing outside of the uterus.

Some people choose a more permanent form of birth control. A woman may have her fallopian tubes sealed off so that the egg cannot pass down into the uterus. This is called a **tubal ligation**. A man can have a **vasectomy** in which each vas deferens is cut and tied so that sperm cannot be ejaculated. These operations do not affect a man or woman's sexual feelings. In some cases the operations can be reversed if the person decides he or she wants to have more children after all.

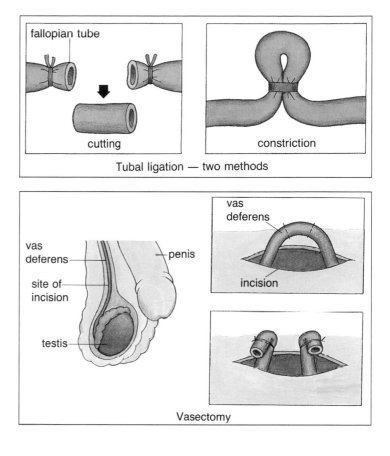

Tubal ligation — two methods

Vasectomy

No form of contraception is 100 percent effective (except abstinence—not having sex). When a woman becomes pregnant but is not able to take on the responsibility of raising a child, she may be faced with a difficult dilemma. Should she try to raise a child under intolerable circumstances, should she give the child up for adoption when it is born, or should she end the pregnancy? This is an important and often complicated moral and emotional decision. A woman may also consider ending a pregnancy if she has been raped or if her unborn child has a genetic disease.

Although extremely controversial and not usually considered a form of birth control, **abortion** is a procedure for ending an unwanted pregnancy. It is simplest and safest when performed within a month or so after conception. Early in pregnancy, abortion can be produced with a surgical device that applies suction to the uterine cavity; at later stages a D and C (dilatation and curettage) operation is performed. Recently, RU-486, a drug that causes the body to abort a fetus without surgery, has been developed.

HELPING PEOPLE WITH REPRODUCTIVE PROBLEMS

Researchers have found many ways to help people prevent having children that they do not want. But there are many couples who want very much to have children but cannot have any. About one out of ten married couples is unable to have children. Researchers are also searching for ways to help them.

One of the most common infertility problems (when a couple cannot conceive a child) occurs when a woman's body does not release an ovum each month. Some drugs can help ova to mature and leave the ovaries. Many women today who have babies could not have had them without these fertility drugs. But sometimes the drugs work too well. They can cause two or three or even more ova to develop at the same time. If all these eggs are fertilized, the woman will have several babies at a time. Most quadruplets and quintuplets that are born these days are cases where the mothers had taken fertility drugs.

Sometimes a couple cannot have a baby because the man is not able to make enough sperm to fertilize the egg. The problem might be simple to fix. Certain lifestyle factors can lead to a decreased amount of sperm,

Fertility drugs can help some women to have children but may cause them to have several babies at one time.

including smoking or drinking too much alcohol, using marijuana or other drugs, taking too much aspirin, or even wearing clothes that are too tight (this causes the temperature in the scrotum to be too high for sperm to mature). If changing these factors does not work, a couple may carefully plot out the time of month when fertilization is most likely to occur and plan sexual intercourse at the optimum times.

If a couple is unable to conceive on their own they may ask a doctor to help. Doctors can save a man's sperm and place them in the woman's body just at the right time to fertilize the egg. This is called **artificial insemination**. Sometimes the sperm are not strong or healthy enough to swim to the egg. A hormone called a prostaglandin has been used to help here.

But sometimes nothing works. If the couple still wants children very much, sperm may be taken from another man, who is not married to the woman. She never meets him or even knows who he is, but his sperm fertilizes her egg and a normal baby is born through artificial insemination. There are sperm banks in which human semen is stored until someone wishes to use it for artificial insemination.

Another approach is called **embryo transfer**. If a woman is unable to produce eggs, her husband's sperm can be used to fertilize another woman's egg in the laboratory. Then the fertilized egg is placed into the womb of the woman who was trying to conceive, where it develops until it is born. In some cases embryos produced from donor eggs have been transferred to women past menopause, who were given hormone treatments to allow their bodies to support a pregnancy.

Another option is to find a **surrogate mother**. This is someone who is artificially inseminated with sperm from the husband of a couple trying to conceive. The surrogate mother carries the baby until it is born and then gives the baby to the couple unable to conceive a child. Surrogacy is very controversial and is illegal in some states, because disputes sometimes arise as to whose baby it really is.

In a relatively new procedure, a few women long past menopause have become pregnant when given high doses of hormones to prepare the uterus for a fertilized egg. The hormone treatments must continue throughout pregnancy. In one case, the egg was supplied by a donor and was fertilized in vitro by the woman's husband. In another case, however, the hormone treatment stimulated the woman's ovaries to release eggs.

REPRODUCTION IN THE FUTURE

In science fiction stories, babies no longer develop inside their mothers. Instead they are grown in test-tubes and float in carefully controlled tanks until they are fully developed. This is still purely fiction, but in England in 1978 the first human baby was born that had been fertilized outside of her mother's body. Several eggs were removed from the mother and placed in a petri dish. Then the father's sperm were added. Fertilization occurred, and two days later one of the eggs was placed back in the mother's uterus. This procedure is called **in vitro fertilization**. Test-tube babies are thus a reality today, but the procedure is still very difficult and expensive. It doesn't seem very likely that this will be a comon method of reproduction in the future.

Another popular reproductive idea in science fiction books is **cloning**—producing an identical twin from a single cell. Theoretically, since practically every cell in your body contains all of your genetic instructions, your identical twin could be created using any of these cells. To clone a person who looks just like you, the nucleus from a skin cell on your fin-

In this example of in vitro fertilization, sperm are added to several eggs in the petri dish in an attempt to fertilize them.

ger could be placed into a human egg which had had its nucleus removed. Then the egg would be placed in a woman's womb. The growing fetus would contain the instructions to produce a carbon copy of you. Although this sounds like farfetched science fiction, forms of cloning have already been done with frogs and mice. So far, though, researchers have not yet succeeded in using cells from adult animals. The cells that supply the genetic instructions are usually taken from embryos.

Science does not yet have the ability to clone a human, but in all probability we will someday have the knowledge needed to do so. When that happens, there will undoubtedly be a lot of controversy about the moral and ethical questions involved in playing creator. Will we someday have a world where everyone looks the same? Scientists will be able to separate X- and Y-carrying sperm. As we learn more about how to change the genetic instructions that make us who we are, will parents try to custom-make children of the sex that they want with all of the qualities that they desire? In India and other Third World countries, many people are already using sonograms to determine the sex of a fetus and are aborting females, who are less valued in their culture. Will musical creativity or artistic ability or mathematical genius be able to be cloned? Remember, environmental factors also come into play in making people who they are.

These are just a few of the problems that we must face as science becomes more involved in helping people decide how and when a new baby will be born.

GLOSSARY

abortion—a procedure for ending an unwanted pregnancy, by surgery or with drugs that induce uterine contractions.

AIDS—acquired immune deficiency syndrome; an STD caused by the human immunodeficiency virus (HIV), which attacks the cells of the body's disease-fighting system and can lead to death from infections; also spread by blood transfusions or sharing infected IV needles for drug abuse.

amniocentesis—withdrawal and testing of a sample of amniotic fluid for genetic diseases.

amniotic sac—the membrane that surrounds the developing embryo, which floats in amniotic fluid.

androgens—male sex hormones.

artificial insemination—the insertion of semen into a woman's uterus by means other than sexual intercourse.

asexual reproduction—reproduction with only one parent.

binary fission—reproduction by splitting into two (usually equal) parts.

birth control pills (or **contraceptive pills**)—drugs that prevent the secretion of hormones triggering ovulation.

blastocyst—an early stage of embryonic development: a two-layered, fluid-filled hollow ball of cells.

breech birth—birth in which the baby's feet or buttocks are the first to enter the birth canal.

budding—reproduction by the production of a smaller duplicate, which may separate from the parent organism.

cervical cap—a small cup-shaped device worn over the cervix to prevent pregnancy.

cervix—the lower, narrow end of the uterus, which opens into the vagina.

cesarean section (or **C-section**)—surgical removal of a baby from the uterus.

chlamydia—an STD caused by a bacterium.

chromosome—a long, threadlike strand of nucleic acids, containing genes. At certain stages of the cell cycle, the chromosomes are coiled into rodlike structures with characteristic shapes that can be recognized on micrographs. In sexual reproduction, an offspring receives half of the complete set of chromosomes from each parent.

cilia—hairlike structures on cells that wave back and forth to create a current in the surrounding fluid.

circumcision—surgical removal of the foreskin.

clitoris—a small structure within the vulva in females that resembles the male penis.

cloning—the production of an identical twin from a single body cell.

condom—a protective latex sheath worn over the penis during intercourse to prevent pregnancy or protect against STDs.

contraceptive—birth control drug or device.

corpus luteum—the progesterone-secreting remains of a burst ovarian follicle.

diaphragm—a cup-shaped device worn over the opening to the uterus to prevent pregnancy.

dilation—widening of an opening (for example, of the cervix during birth).

dominant—in genetics, a characteristic (trait) that will appear in the offspring even if only one gene for it is present.

egg—an ovum; female sex cell. In a fertilized egg, a male sex cell (sperm) has joined with the ovum.

ejaculation—the ejection of semen from the penis during sexual activity.

ejaculatory ducts—tubes through which sperm pass out of the penis.

embryo—an immature form of an organism, produced by sexual reproduction.

embryo transfer—the insertion of a fertilized donor egg into the uterus of an infertile woman.

endometriosis—a condition in which endometrial tissue grows in the body cavity and periodically thickens then sloughs off and bleeds.

endometrium—the lining of the uterus.

epididymis—collecting tube leading out of a seminiferous tubule.

erection—a swelling and firming-up of the penis that aids in inserting it into the woman's reproductive tract.

estrogens—female sex hormones.

estrous cycle—in mammals, periodic times of "heat" when the female is receptive to mating.

fallopian tubes—tubes through which ova pass from the ovaries to the uterus. Also called oviducts.

fertilization—the joining of male and female sex cells to form a new organism. External fertilization occurs outside the body; internal fertilization occurs inside the body of the female. Self-fertilization is the production of offspring by a single organism with both male and female sex organs.

fetal alcohol syndrome—a combination of low birth weight and physical and mental defects in a baby born to a woman who abused alcohol during pregnancy.

fetus—a human embryo after the ninth week of development.

foreskin—a loose fold of skin that protects the glans of the penis.

fraternal twins—two babies that develop and are born at the same time but came from two different fertilized eggs.

gamete—a special sex cell that joins with another gamete of the opposite sex to produce a new organism.

genes—units of heredity, containing the instructions for a particular trait, coded in the form of nucleic acids.

genetics—the study of heredity.

genital—pertaining to the reproductive structures.

genital herpes—an STD caused by herpes simplex virus Type 2.

gestation—the period of prenatal development.

glans—the cap-shaped tip of the penis.

gonads—sex organs.

gonorrhea—an STD caused by a bacterium.

gynecologist—a doctor who specializes in the female reproductive organs.

hepatitis—liver inflammation; hepatitis B, caused by a virus, can be transmitted sexually or by blood and is a major cause of death.

hermaphrodite—an animal possessing both male and female sex organs.

homosexuality—a preference for members of one's own sex as love and sex partners.

hymen—a thin sheet of tissue that covers the opening of the vagina.

hypospadias—a malformation of the penis in which the underside did not close completely during prenatal development.

hysterectomy—surgical removal of the uterus, sometimes with the ovaries and fallopian tubes as well.

identical twins—two babies developed from a single fertilized egg. They have identical sets of genes and are always of the same sex.

impotence—inability of a male to sustain an erection and engage in sexual intercourse.

infertility—an inability to conceive (become pregnant), usually due to failure to ovulate or blockage of the fallopian tubes.

in vitro fertilization—the fertilization of a ripe ovum with sperm in a laboratory dish. The embryo is then transferred to the uterus of a woman prepared for implantation by hormone injections.

IUD (intrauterine device)—a device inserted into the uterus that prevents implantation of an embryo.

labia—two pairs of skin flaps that surround the vaginal opening.

labor—the birth process, in which the cervix dilates and contractions of the uterus gradually expel the baby.

mammary glands—the milk-producing glands in the breasts.

mammogram—an X-ray picture of the breast.

mastectomy—surgical removal of the breast, sometimes with other tissues.

meiosis—division of sex cells, resulting in gametes with half the normal number of chromosomes.

menopause—the cessation of functioning of a woman's reproductive system.

menstrual cycle—the monthly maturation and release of an ovum, coordinated with the preparation of the uterus to support growth of an embryo.

mitosis—cell division, forming two identical cells, each containing the same number of chromosomes as the parent.

morning sickness—nausea felt by some women during the first trimester of pregnancy.

obstetrician—a doctor specializing in delivering babies and caring for pregnant women.

orgasm—muscular contractions of the genital organs and intense feelings of pleasure at the climax of sexual activity; in males it is combined with ejaculation.

osteoporosis—thinning and weakening of the bones, which may occur during aging.

ovarian follicle—the estrogen-secreting sac in which an ovum matures.

ovary—a structure in which female sex cells (ova) are produced.

ovulation—release of a mature ovum from an ovary.

ovum—a female sex cell; an egg. (Plural: ova.)

oxytocin—a hormone that stimulates uterine contractions during and after birth and also stimulates the release of milk from the breasts.

Pap smear—a test for cancer of tissue samples from the vagina and cervix.

parthenogenesis—a variation of sexual reproduction in which female offspring are produced without mating.

pelvic inflammatory disease (PID)—an infection of the female reproductive system that is caused by several bacteria.

penis—the male reproductive organ, which transfers sperm to the female.

period (or **menstrual period**)—the menstrual blood flow that occurs when the uterine lining is shed.

pistil—the female organ of a flower.

placenta—a structure in mammals that provides nourishment for a growing embryo and removes its waste products by an exchange with the mother's bloodstream.

PMS (premenstrual syndrome)—a condition of irritability, depression, headaches, and bloating experienced by some women before or during their menstrual period.

pollen—dustlike particles containing the male sex cells of a flower.

pollination—the transfer of pollen from the male organs of a flower to the female organ of the same or another flower of the same species.

polyembryony—the birth of more than one baby at once.

pregnancy—the condition of carrying a developing embryo or fetus.

prenatal—referring to the time before birth.

progesterone—a female sex hormone that prepares the body for pregnancy.

prostate gland—a structure surrounding the ejaculatory ducts that produces some of the components of semen.

puberty—the period of maturation of the sex organs.

recessive—in genetics, a characteristic (trait) that will not appear in the offspring unless two genes for it are present.

reproduction—the production by living organisms of more of their own kind.

scrotum (or scrotal sac)—the loose bag of skin containing the testes.

secondary sex characteristics—structural differences determined by sex but not directly related to the reproductive function—such as amount of muscle development, amount and distribution of body hair, fat deposits, voices, and pelvic structure.

semen—sperm-containing fluid that is transferred from the male to the female during sexual intercourse.

seminiferous tubules—tiny coiled tubes in the testes that produce sperm.

sex chromosomes—a pair of chromosomes that determine sex. (A female has two X chromosomes; a male has one X and one Y chromosome.)

sex hormones—chemicals that stimulate sexual maturation and aid in reproduction.

sexual intercourse—the insertion of the male's penis into the female's vagina (vaginal intercourse) for reproduction, for the pleasurable sensations that accompany it, or as an expression of love and intimacy. Nonreproductive variations include oral intercourse (insertion of the male's penis into his partner's mouth) and anal intercourse (insertion of the male's penis into his partner's anus).

sexual reproduction—reproduction by two parents of different sexes.

Siamese twins—identical twins who developed from a single fertilized egg that did not separate completely. They may share limbs and organs.

sperm—male sex cells.

sporulation—asexual reproduction by the production of one-celled spores.

stamens—the male organs of a flower.

STDs—sexually transmitted diseases; also called venereal diseases.

sterility—an inability to produce children (in males, usually due to insufficient production of sperm).

surrogate mother—a woman who is artificially inseminated and bears a child for an infertile couple.

syphilis—an STD caused by a bacterium; if untreated can lead to severe heart and lung damage, dementia, and death.

testis—structure in male animals in which sperm are produced. (Plural: testes.)

testosterone—the major male sex hormone.

toxic shock syndrome—a rare, severe illness that has been traced to the use of tampons to absorb menstrual flow.

trimesters—the three parts of pregnancy, each three months long.

tubal ligation—a surgical procedure in which the fallopian tubes are cut and tied off, preventing the passage of ova into the uterus.

ultrasound sonography—the use of high-frequency ultrasound to produce a picture of the developing fetus inside the uterus.

umbilical cord—a cord of tissue, containing blood vessels, that connects the developing embryo to its mother's uterus.

uterus—the structure in which a female mammal's offspring develop; the womb.

vagina—a muscular-walled tube that serves as the entrance to the female reproductive tract.

vaginal sponge—a device used to block the vaginal passage during intercourse to prevent pregnancy.

vas deferens—the sperm duct, a tube leading from the epididymis into the penis.

vasectomy—a surgical procedure in which each vas deferens is cut and tied to prevent ejaculation of sperm.

vernix caseosa—a greasy white substance that covers the skin of a newborn baby.

vulva—the female external sex organs.

yolk—material in an egg used to nourish the embryo.

zygote—the fertilized egg, a combination of ovum and sperm.

TIMELINE

INDEX